THAILAND

Philippe Bénet

CONTENTS

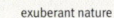 exuberant nature

3	This Way Thailand
7	Flashback
15	On the Scene
15	Bangkok
33	Gulf of Thailand and Andaman Sea
51	The Centre
55	The North
65	Northern Tribes
71	Dining Out
75	Shopping
79	Sports
83	The Hard Facts
88	Index

Features
- 10 Buddhism
- 16 The Royal Family
- 61 Poi Sang Long Festival
- 69 The Karen and their Elephants

Maps
- 28 Ayutthaya
- 46 Phuket

Fold-out map
Thailand
Bangkok Centre
Bangkok

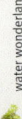 water wonderland

strong workforce

 Land of smiles

THIS WAY THAILAND

Thailand is shaped roughly like an elephant's head, the top butting the mountains of the north, in the region of the Golden Triangle, the trunk plunging into the blue waters of the Gulf of Thailand all the way to the Malay Peninsula in the south. To the east, an ear flaps over a vast plateau bordered by the Mekong. The teeming capital, Bangkok, lies in the animal's mouth.

Before 1939, the country was called Siam, a kingdom founded in the 13th century. As it had never been colonized, it was renamed Muang Thai, "Land of the Free". Today Thailand is a constitutional monarchy comprising 75 *jangwaat* (provinces) and the administrative area of Bangkok. The people hold their sovereign in great esteem. Crowned in 1950, His Majesty King Bhumibol Adulyadej (Rama IX) is the ninth king of the Chakri dynasty, founded in 1782.

Almost a quarter of the 64 million inhabitants are under 15 years of age, and about 65 per cent work in agriculture. The population is an extraordinary mix composed of Thais (75 per cent), Chinese (14 per cent), Malays (4 per cent) and many minority groups. More than 90 per cent of the population practise Buddhism, a fact that penetrates daily life to the core. Even in the sophisticated capital, women turn out in front of their houses soon after dawn to offer rice to saffron-robed monks.

Temples and Beaches

Thailand delights every taste, aesthetic, eccentric or exotic. There's so much to see and do, you may barely find time for a swim. In tumultuous Bangkok, catch your breath in the serene atmosphere of a temple. Then experience the passing of time as you glide along the Chao Phraya River in a boat, observing the life of the canals, the colonial quarter with the legendary Oriental Hotel, and the futuristic skyscrapers. Take time to wander around Chinatown, where the odours of the opium dens and brothels still linger. But times have changed. Children whose parents rode water buffaloes out in the rice fields now

The warmth of Thai hospitality reflected in a smile.

programme computers and run production lines. In turn, city dwellers have to travel more than 100 km (60 miles) to find an authentic floating market.

The south, with its coral-studded islands set in crystalline waters, is a haven of peace and tranquillity. The sparkling sand, blue sky and emerald sea make Phuket a perfect island retreat. Nature-lovers shouldn't miss the limestone cliffs of Phang Nga Bay, while Ko Samui in the Gulf of Thailand offers long white beaches and coconut groves.

Mountains and Hill Tribes

The north preserves an inscrutable charm. The landscape is very different from the south, with fertile plains, mountainous areas and waterfalls. The lush countryside produces everything from rice to the most prized exotic fruits, and flowers from frangipane to orchids. The poppy plantations have been converted to less controversial crops, but the Golden Triangle remains nevertheless an international hub of drug traffic. You may not actually meet any smugglers or overlords, but your imagination will fill in the details.

More conventional sightseeing covers historic towns, Buddhist temples, palaces, gardens—and training camps for elephants. The cities of northern Thailand are springboards for expeditions into the country of the hill tribes, some still living in the Stone Age, with a rare talent for art and crafts. Their numbers have been increased in recent years with the arrival of communities driven by war out of Cambodia and Myanmar (previously Burma).

A Sense of Welcome

It's fascinating to travel in this land of teak and elephants, where rice and tolerance are cultivated with equal enthusiasm. If many foreigners have chosen to settle here, it's because they appreciate the perfect balance between exoticism, tradition and pageantry on the one hand and kindness, comfort and a genuine welcome on the other. The wisdom of the Thai people is based on respect for the monarchy, the family and religion.

The tourist infrastructure is sophisticated. In luxury hotels and modest inns alike, you'll meet with a genuine welcome and a high standard of cleanliness. Connections all across the country, by air-conditioned luxury coach, by rail or by air, are very practical and convenient. And security can be taken for granted. In Thailand, the tourist is king, welcomed by a hospitable, warm-hearted people. There's so much to see that there'll be plenty to discover next time you come.

A banyan has imprisoned a sandstone head of Buddha at Ayutthaya.

FLASHBACK

The Mon people established kingdoms across today's Thailand from the 6th to the 11th centuries. Known as the Dvaravati civilization, they came under Indian influence through trade and practised Theravada Buddhism, leaving behind some interesting bronze and sandstone Buddhas. From the northeast, the Khmer empire extended its dominion, as shown by the presence of imposing temples such as Phimai. During the 11th century, the Angkor kingdom succeeded in annexing Mon territory.

The Thai people, from Yunnan in southern China, infiltrated in successive waves. They founded Chiang Rai, Chiang Mai, Lamphun and Sukhothai. In the 13th century they drove out the Khmer, who pulled back to the northeast.

Thai Kingdom

The Thais settled in the plain of Menam Chao Phraya where they founded the kingdom of Sukhothai. Rama Khamhaeng (1277–1317) extended his territory to Luang Prabang (in present-day Laos) and the Malay Peninsula, establishing diplomatic relations, creating the Thai written language and setting up the first monetary system. Under the reign of this enlightened monarch, a national identity began to emerge.

One of his successors, King Rama Thibodi, founded the city of Ayutthaya in 1350, in a fertile region at the confluence of the rivers which form the Menam Chao Phraya. Thanks to successive expansions towards Pegu (Myanmar), Angkor and Chiang Mai, this kingdom would eventually stretch across the entire Chao Phraya basin towards the Mekong and the Gulf of Siam.

Traditionally patrons and protectors of the arts, the Thai sovereigns opened their kingdom to foreigners and in 1511 began developing trade with the Portuguese, who were gradually supplanted by the Dutch. English traders arrived in Siam very early in the 16th century.

The eternal conflict between implacable enemies, the Khmer

and the Burmese, took a dramatic turn for Siam at the end of the 18th century. On April 7, 1767, after more than a year of siege, the Burmese invaded, looted and burned the capital Ayutthaya, taking 90,000 prisoners.

A few hundred men, led by the General (and future king) Taksin (1768–82) managed to escape and settle in Thonburi, on the opposite side of the river from modern Bangkok. From there, they waged a war of attrition against the Burmese, from whom they recaptured the cities of Chiang Mai, Luang Prabang and finally Ayutthaya. King Taksin, who had descended into madness, was assassinated in 1782.

Chakri Dynasty

Taksin was succeeded by General Chakri, victor over the Burmese. He was the founder of the Chakri dynasty, which still reigns in Thailand today. Taking the title of Rama I (1782–1809), he set up his capital in Krung Thep or "City of Angels", today's Bangkok. He built numerous palaces and temples similar to those which were the glory of Ayutthaya, re-established Buddhism as the state religion and codified the law. His successors managed to stabilize the kingdom.

King Mongkut (Rama IV, 1851–68), the ruler portrayed in *The King and I*, acceded to the throne at the age of 47, having spent more than 20 years of his life in a monastery. He followed with interest the beginnings of the Industrial Revolution in the West and launched a huge programme to build roads and canals throughout the land.

Mongkut's son King Chulalongkorn (Rama V, 1868–1910) was the enlightened monarch the country had been waiting for. He received a bilingual education and had a profound admiration for Great Britain. During the 42 years of his reign, he continued his father's innovative ideas, modernizing his kingdom with intelligence and instituting major reforms in every domain—the abolition of slavery, development of education and the creation of high schools for the most able, establishment of law courts and reform of the judiciary. He also ordered vast projects to improve the road and rail infrastructure.

In 1892, he nominated a Western-style government of 12 ministers under the authority of a prime minister. His Cambridge-educated son Vajiravudh (Rama VI, 1910–25) continued the advances made by his father, but with somewhat less success. During World War I, Thailand sided with the Allies. But the Crash of 1929 led to the imposition of austerity measures which caused frustration among the elite, whose members had imported democratic ideas from Europe. Two of these men, Pridi Phanomyong and Phibul Songkhram, both educated in France, came to the fore.

A coup d'état on June 24, 1932, instituted a constitutional monarchy. The king was exiled to Great Britain and abdicated in 1935 in favour of his ten-year-old nephew Ananda Mahidol. Power devolved upon Phibul, who in 1939 changed the country's name from Siam to Thailand.

During the War in the Pacific, Japan forced Thailand to declare war on the United States and Great Britain. A resistance movement was organized under the leadership of Pridi Phanomyong, who assumed power at the Liberation. But a drama was soon to upset Thai politics: on June 9, 1946, King Ananda was found shot dead in Bangkok. Pridi Phanomyong was falsely accused of regicide and went into exile. His brother Bhumibol Adulyadej inherited the throne as Rama IX.

Henceforth and until 1974, the government remained in the hands of the military, first under Marshal Phibul and then under General Sarit Thanarat. Faced with a number of student demonstrations demanding a new constitution, and a series of strikes which paralysed the country, the army opted for repression. On October 14, 1973, tanks fired into the crowd, killing more than 300 and wounding over 1000 demonstrators. The disaster prompted the resignation of the military government, but not for long. The civilian rulers proved to be incapable of governing, and the army reclaimed power on October 6, 1976, citing the dangers of communism. One leader, General Prem Tinsulanonda, ruled from 1979 until 1988. In 1992 a coalition government was formed. Dr Thaksin Shinawatra of the Thai Rak Thai party was elected in 2001 and 2005. In September 2006 he was ousted by a peaceful military coup. In December 2007 Samak Sundaravej, leader of the PPP (People's Power Party), was elected prime minister, but was forced to resign a year later, on corruption charges. The opposition leader Abhisit Vejjajiva was elected in 2008.

Originally from southern China, the Meo or Hmong settled around Chiang Mai, where they cultivate rice, maize and garlic.

BUDDHISM

The spirit of Buddha (his name means "the Enlightened One") is omnipresent. With the first rays of the morning sun, you can observe the everyday but uplifting sight of bonzes and novices (who number 5 million in all) passing through towns and villages in silence and in single file, wooden bowl in hand, begging for their daily bread. The Thais await them in front of their houses to offer rice or curry wrapped in banana leaves, then bow to thank the monks for this opportunity of doing a *tham boun*, a worthy deed which will be taken into account in their next life.

More than 90 per cent of the population are practising Buddhists. Thailand has 100,000 temples and 30,000 monasteries, home to 10 per cent of the male population. Every Thai male is expected to withdraw for two or three months during his adolescence to a *wat* (monastery) where he leads the life of a bonze. The *buot nag* (ordination ceremony), a ritual as compulsory as a wedding or a funeral, symbolizes Buddha's farewell to the world. The future novice, dressed as a prince, leaves the home of his parents for the monastery. His head and eyebrows shaven, his nails trimmed, he passes through the village on horseback or by car, accompanied by musicians and dancers, before

Renata Holzbachová

entering the *wat* where he will put on the saffron robe. Within, he will receive a good education, learn to meditate and observe no fewer than 227 rules of life.

Buddhists believe in reincarnation. After death everyone is held to be reincarnated as a human being, a sage or an animal, according to his or her karma, the balance sheet of his or her virtuous or evil deeds. Buddha offers the means to escape these endless cycles of reincarnation *(samsara)* and to reach nirvana, the state of supreme wisdom. Buddhism is in fact more of a philosophy than a religion. Although Buddha is in charge of the population's highest aspirations, in daily life the people turn to more ancient spirits who are invoked to provide rain, better harvests or even children. Before each house, a small altar shows that guardian spirits are present to watch over the family. The Thais are superstitious: many wear amulets or tattoos believed to ward off evil and they are regular visitors to the consulting rooms of astrologers.

The Story of Buddha

The life of Prince Siddhartha Gautama, who lived in the 6th century bc, began with a prediction. It had been announced to King Suddhodana, whose kingdom was in Nepal, that his son would become either an emperor or an ascetic who would renounce all his worldly goods after encounters with a sick man, an old man, a corpse and a monk. Fearing the second hypothesis, the king arranged a very sheltered upbringing for Gautama, who at 16 years of age married a beautiful princess. A few years later, the prince requested his father's permission to leave the palace, and the king consented, but not without ordering the guards to remove from Gautama's path anything which might fulfil the prophecy. But to no avail: Gautama became aware of suffering and death. Travelling through the valley of the Ganges for six years, he became an ascetic and renounced worldly pleasures at the age of 35.

Temples and Monasteries

The temples and monasteries are meeting places for all generations and all social classes. In each village, life centres on the *wat*, a group of buildings acting as monastery, Buddhist temple and school, but also as a parish hall and community centre open to everyone. Ordination ceremonies take place in the *bot*, the faithful and

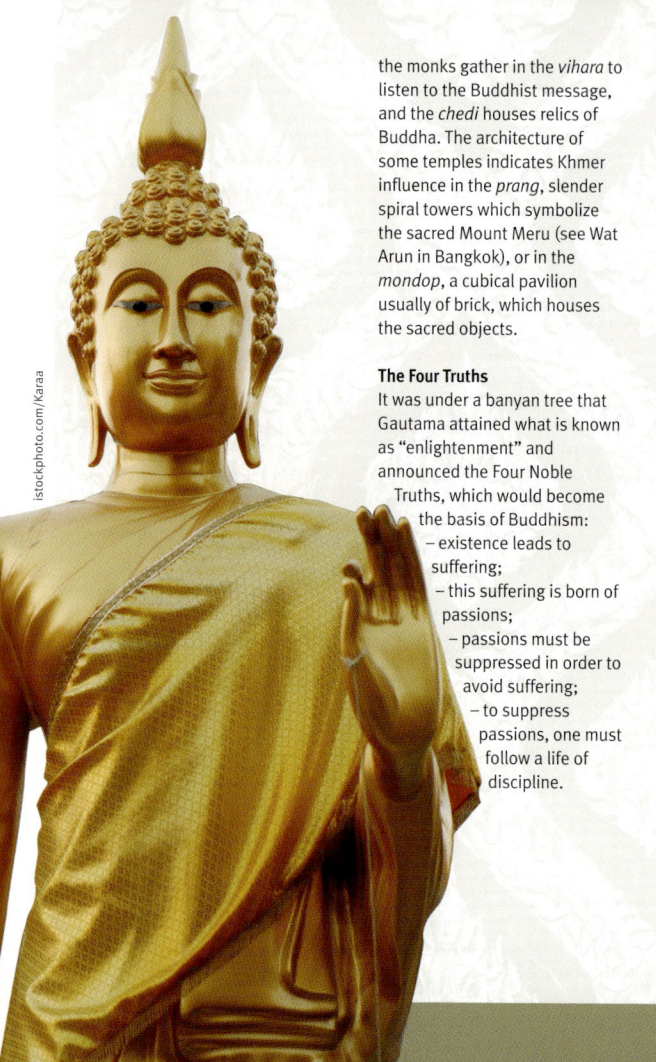

the monks gather in the *vihara* to listen to the Buddhist message, and the *chedi* houses relics of Buddha. The architecture of some temples indicates Khmer influence in the *prang*, slender spiral towers which symbolize the sacred Mount Meru (see Wat Arun in Bangkok), or in the *mondop*, a cubical pavilion usually of brick, which houses the sacred objects.

The Four Truths
It was under a banyan tree that Gautama attained what is known as "enlightenment" and announced the Four Noble Truths, which would become the basis of Buddhism:
– existence leads to suffering;
– this suffering is born of passions;
– passions must be suppressed in order to avoid suffering;
– to suppress passions, one must follow a life of discipline.

THE POSITIONS OF BUDDHA

Statues show Buddha in various traditional positions (standing, seated, walking and reclining), with different hand gestures *(mudra)*. The four principal poses are as follows.

The **Abhaya (1)** mudra shows Buddha standing, one hand outstretched with the palm facing out. He is taming evil forces, dispelling fear and bestowing blessings

In the **Dhyana (2)** mudra, the seated Buddha's hands rest on his legs, which are folded in the lotus position. This symbolizes meditation.

The **Bhumisparsa (3)** mudra depicts Buddha seated in the lotus position, his right hand touching the right knee, which represents the ground, and his left hand on his legs. Here Buddha is meditating beneath a banyan tree, having vowed not to move until he receives enlightenment. However, the demon Mara tries to distract him, so Buddha is calling the earth to witness his vow.

Lastly, the reclining position **(4)** does not depict Buddha sleeping, but at the moment when he attains nirvana.

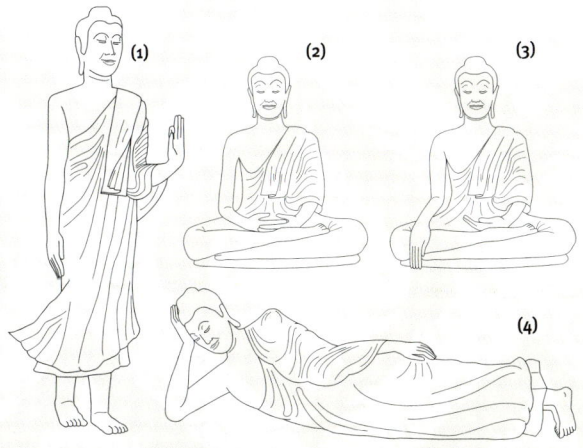

The modern showcases the traditional in the heart of Bangkok.

ON THE SCENE

In Thailand, all roads lead to Bangkok, the nation's seething capital. Even if you're heading elsewhere, plan to spend a few days there; its temples should not be missed—and its food is the best in the land. The rest of the country offers enough variety to satisfy every taste. For luxurious facilities, go to Phuket. If you want to commune with nature, you will love Ko Phi Phi. In search of solitude—go to Ko Tao. Ko Samui will please those who like lots of activities. Hikers will prefer the mountainous north, starting out at Chiang Mai and meeting some of the region's fascinating tribespeople.

The royal heart of Bangkok nestles in a curve of the Chao Phraya River, grouping the city's main attractions—the Royal Palace, the Temple of the Emerald Buddha (Wat Phra Kaeo), Wat Pho and the National Museum. Many other sights are contained in the oval area bounded by Krung Kasem Road and the river (originally an island): Chinatown and the Thieves' Market, a number of temples and monuments. You can take a fast boat to the colonial quarter, past the French Embassy, the Oriental Hotel and the cathedral, stopping off on your return journey at the base of Wat Arun, whose silhouette is visible from afar.

To enjoy Bangkok in comfort, get up early and take advantage of the cool morning air; the atmosphere soon becomes stifling in the dry season.

Royal Bangkok

After the Burmese destroyed the capital, Ayutthaya, General Taksin set up his new headquarters in Thonburi, a trading centre founded in 1557 on the south bank of the Chao Phraya River, opposite modern Bangkok. Taksin's successor Rama I made Bangkok the new capital of the country and gave it the name of Krung Thep ("City of Angels"). The island of Ratanakosin was chosen as the site of the Grand

THE ROYAL FAMILY

Crowned in 1950, King Bhumibol Adulyadej (Rama IX) was married that same year to "the very beautiful Sirikit", as the Thais call her. Whereas political coalitions have come and gone, the popularity of the king, the sacred symbol of the nation, has remained constant. He presides over the transformation of his kingdom into one of Asia's Tiger economies, while endeavouring to retain its traditional values. Whenever he appears on television, or when the Thai national anthem booms out of loudspeakers, the Thais stop in their tracks and stand to attention.

Although the king has no real power, his presence is reassuring when political manoeuvring or corruption threaten the nation's stability. He played an important part as mediator during the 1973 disturbances and again during the political crisis of 1992, when a coalition government was formed. Never without his camera, he travels around the country, visiting the poorest regions, offering words of comfort to the destitute and giving donations to charitable organizations. He has been involved in a vast project to bring artificial rain to the drought-stricken northeast, while the queen led a campaign to preserve regional handicrafts, wearing silk outfits made by designers from the north. She has encouraged the northern peoples to continue producing jewellery, and created a foundation for the promotion of arts and crafts. Princess Mara Chakri Sirindhorn, born in 1955, is active in the fight against AIDS.

Palace and Royal Chapel, built to house the Emerald Buddha brought back from Laos. The seat of political and cultural power was installed here. King Chulalongkorn, or Rama V, began to modernize of Thailand after visiting Europe, and the capital suddenly began to develop. Ratchadamnoen Klang, a wide, leafy boulevard similar to the Champs Elysées, was laid out, followed by other broad avenues in the European style. Italian architects were summoned to design the new palaces, and Chinese rickshaws plied the streets before cars appeared on the scene in 1902. The city centre is intersected by concentric canals, or *klongs*, busy with boat traffic.

Grand Palace

In the centre of the river's curve, crenellated walls enclose the Grand Palace and Wat Phra Kaeo, the Temple of the Emerald Buddha. The palace is no longer the residence of the royal family, but visitors are expected to show respect and dress modestly (no shorts or bare arms).

The Grand Palace was founded by Rama I in 1783 and designed to resemble its counterpart in Ayutthaya, with royal apartments, reception rooms and harem. The existing buildings, a mixture of Thai and Victorian architecture, were built by Rama V in 1867.

A number of smaller buildings at the entrance to the Grand Palace are worthy of note. The first is **Chakri Maha Prasat**, with a long neoclassical façade and surmounted by a *chedi* (shrine). The king receives ambassadors in the throne room, at the centre of the building. The inner palace used to be closed to the outside world. Some 3000 women lived here during the reign of Rama V. Girls from aristocratic families and female servants were given a refined education here. You can visit several of the palace rooms.

In the main courtyard, there's a **Chinese topiary garden** planted with ebony trees.

The Audience Hall of **Dusit Maha Prasat** has a four-storey roof; the mortal remains of members of the royal family lie in state here before cremation.

Another group of buildings, Phra Maha Monthien, includes the coronation hall, **Phra Thinang Phaisan Taksin**.

A coin museum is housed in the **Pavilion of Royal Decorations and Numismatics**; its displays include the crown jewels, gold swords, coins and other means of payment used in Thailand since the 11th century.

Wat Phra Kaeo

Guarded by demonic, ogre-like statues, *yaksa*, which keep evil spirits at bay, the Temple of the

Emerald Buddha was built in 1782 by Rama I and modelled on the royal temple of the Grand Palace in Ayutthaya. Every visitor is inevitably dazzled by the incredible profusion of gold and sumptuous mosaics in vivid colours. Nothing is too fine for the Emerald Buddha, a small statue 66 cm (26 inches) tall, 48 cm (19 inches) wide, carved from a single block of green jasper and credited with magical powers. The temple serves as the king's private chapel; he comes here three times a year with the changes of the season to bring ritual offerings to the Buddha. He also brings a tunic of symbolic importance: one of diamonds and gold for the hot season, blue for the rainy season, and for the cool season, enamel and gold.

The origins of the Emerald Buddha are unknown. It was discovered at Chiang Rai in 1434, in a *chedi* that had been destroyed by lightning. The statue was covered with a layer of stucco which flaked off to reveal the translucent green stone within. The king of Chiang Mai organized an expedition to fetch the statue, but the elephant entrusted to carry it back chose, despite the orders of its mahout, to take it to the town of Lampang. It remained there for 32 years, then was carried off to Chiang Mai and afterwards to Luang Prabang in Laos. It was kept there for two centuries, until this temple was built in Bangkok.

Take time to look at the figures of divinities that people the temple surroundings, specially those with male or female heads and torsos and bird's legs and bodies. There are superb murals in the cloister illustrating the exploits of Hanuman, the Monkey King, and hero of *Ramakien*, the Thai version of the *Ramayana*.

Massage and meditation. Wat Pho is the best place in Bangkok for a traditional Thai massage, expertly carried out by professional masseurs.
You can sign up for 30 hours of lessons and obtain a diploma, which is recognized internationally. It is advised to go for a massage in the morning, before you have breakfast. Don't be afraid to try out the many serious salons around town. Foot massage (reflexology) is extremely popular. The body massages can be quite vigorous; advise the masseur beforehand if you have any muscular problems or you are particularly delicate. This service is also offered on the beaches, with a smile, for a reasonable fee.

Lessons in meditation are given three times a day at Wat Mahathat, near the Grand Palace.

Wat Pho

Sanam Chai Road leads south from the Grand Palace to Wat Pho, the Temple of the Reclining Buddha. This is the oldest temple in Bangkok, founded in the 16th century, and Thailand's biggest monastery. Its pavilions, *chedi* and walled gardens fill an area of almost 8 ha (20 acres), in an enclosure pierced by 16 gates. The shrine houses the largest Buddha in the country, a statue 46 m (150 ft) long and 15 m (50 ft) high, representing Buddha in the reclining position that symbolizes the "complete extinction" accompanying nirvana. The body is covered in gold leaf, apart from the soles of the feet, decorated with incrustations of mother-of-pearl representing the 108 distinctive signs of Buddha. The interior of the shrine is adorned with splendid mural frescoes.

This temple is often described as the first university in the land, because Rama III decided to make it a forum for the transmission of knowledge to monks and the population in general. Collections of medicinal plants and of minerals from the various parts of the kingdom were displayed to

A tuk-tuk, the local taxi. | **Brief encounter between two monks and a *kinnari*—half-woman, half-bird, at Wat Phra Kaeo.** | **Wat Pho: painted panel.**

Traditional theatre. In the masked dance known as *khon*, actors play the parts of characters in the *Ramakien*—Rama, the prince, and Sidha, the princess. All the performers in *lakhone* theatre are women. Music accompanies the elegant *rabam* dance, in which the female dancers wear long metal fingernails. Troupes of travelling players stage *likay* theatre, acting scenes based on the feelings and occupations of their contemporaries. *Nang talung* is shadow-puppet theatre, where you see silhouettes of puppets on a screen; they are crafted from bamboo and buffalo hide, manipulated above the heads of the puppeteers. Another form of puppet theatre, with more conventional figurines, is *hun krabok*. Each puppet is controlled by three people.

the public. Mural paintings were designed to cover scientific and cultural topics such as medicine, history, the conduct of war and morality. Several hundred statues, saved from the ruins of Ayutthaya by Rama I, are exhibited in glass cases, and there are galleries around the temple housing 394 Buddhas.

Wat Pho is also a reputed centre for traditional Thai massage *(nuad bo rarn)*—undoubtedly one of the best addresses in the country, along with the school at Chiang Mai. It is open to the public who flock here every day from 8 a.m. to 6 p.m.

National Museum

North of Wat Phra Kaeo is the Pramane esplanade (Sanam Luang), where royal cremations take place, and kite-flying competitions are held. Between here and the river stands the National Museum, one of the finest in South-East Asia. It occupies several buildings in what used to be the Viceroy's palace, until Rama V abolished the post.

The museum is a delight for lovers of ancient history and Buddhist art but can be bewildering, as over a thousand objects are displayed. Consider taking a guided tour to better appreciate the important finds from prehistoric archaeological sites and from the Mon and Khmer kingdoms. Superb statues of Buddha in bronze, clay and stone trace the turbulent history of Buddhism in Thailand. There are also rich and fascinating collections of jewellery, masks and puppets, musical instruments, elephant tusks and several royal palanquins.

National Theatre
Next to the National Museum, the theatre stages Thai classical dramas and international performances, with special exhibition shows of Thai classical dancing and music on the last Friday and Saturday of each month.

National Gallery
Opposite the theatre is the National Gallery, displaying traditional and modern works by Thai artists.

Along the Chao Phraya
Rising in the northern highlands, the Chao Phraya runs for more than 360 km (224 miles), irrigating the Central Plain, which is one of the greatest granaries in all Asia. In Bangkok it becomes a busy thoroughfare, plied by the ferries of the Chao Phraya Express Company from 6 a.m. to 6 p.m. It provides a relatively breezy way of getting to and from the temples of Wat Pho and Wat Arun, the colonial district and the modern city. A shuttle service operates between the palace side of the river and Thonburi. There is also a tourist boat stopping only at the piers of interest to tourists, which functions with a one-day pass.

For a complete change of pace, take a canal boat to float through western Bangkok to observe life by the waterside. You can embark at Tha Thien pier, near Wat Pho.

Royal Barge Museum
Standing over the Bangkok Noi canal (closest river stop is Pin Klao Bridge Pier), an enormous boathouse shelters a number of the superbly carved boats used for royal processions. The most impressive is the royal barge of Rama I: over 45 m (147 ft) in length it required a crew of more than 60 men, including 54 oarsmen—and one minstrel.

Wat Arun
Rama II built the Temple of Dawn on the riverbank at Thonburi in the early 19th century. You can't miss its central spire *(prang)*, especially impressive in the evening when the sun sets behind it. In style, it is characteristic of Khmer temple architecture and symbolizes Mount Meru (the abode of the gods). Inlaid with a glittering mosaic of Chinese porcelain, the *prang* is 74 m (243 ft) tall. The temple served as King Taksin's Royal Chapel and housed the Emerald Buddha

before it was moved to Wat Phra Kaeo. Inside, you can climb the steep steps to the first level for a view over the city and river.

Chinatown and Other Central Sights

Half of Bangkok's population is of Chinese origin. Dynasties have been established through marriage with Thai women, and nowadays they dominate business life in the country.

Chinese Quarter

Yaowarat Road is the centre of Chinatown, a street of goldsmiths and upmarket grocers. It runs parallel with and south of Charoen Krung Road; at the western end, between the two, is the **Nakhon Kasem** district, otherwise known as the Thieves' Market. Sampheng Lane, south again, is a little sleazy; it was once famous for its opium dens and brothels. The Chinese quarter has always been a great place for losing your way; as you stroll around you will come across several Taoist temples. **Wat Traimit**, near the Hualamphong railway station, houses a seated Buddha in solid gold, created during the Sukothai era.

Wat Suthat

Due east of the Grand Palace, the Temple of the Giant Swing was begun during the reign of Rama I and completed in the reign of Rama III. The country's largest bronze Buddha is enshrined here. Don't miss the superb carved door panels, produced in the time of Rama II. Inside, the pillars and walls are beautifully painted. Outside is the tall red-painted teak Sao Ching Cha or Giant Swing, where a Brahmanic ceremony used to take place annually to celebrate the rice harvest. Men would ride the swing and try to grab—with their teeth—a bag of silver coins attached to a pole. This ritual was discontinued in the 1930s after numerous accidents and deaths.

Swallows' Nests. The best restaurants of Bangkok usually feature birds' nest soup on the menu. Resembling translucent Chinese noodles, the main ingredient of this delicacy is the cup-shaped nest that the male Indonesian swallow, *Collocalia fuciphaga,* makes from its saliva during the breeding season. This bird is known locally as *not kin lom,* or "swallower of the wind", and is closely related to the swift. It navigates in the dark using sounds emitted at a frequency of 20 Hz, which echoes off the walls of the cave where it builds its nest. The highly prized white nests are harvested from February to July.

Wat Saket

To the northeast, this rather insignificant temple was built during the reign of Rama I at the foot of the Golden Mount, an artificial hill representing the sacred Mount Meru. Its 318 steps lead up to a gilded *chedi* holding relics of Buddha. There is a beautiful view over the city from the top. Take the time to look at the frescoes in the cloister illustrating the *Ramakien*, and the 17th-century reading room on stilts. In November, a festival is held here, with candle-lit processions.

Opposite the Golden Mount, there's a popular **amulet market** where you can buy charms and talismans, some of them made by Buddhist monks to ensure good luck, fortune or protection against evil.

Democracy Monument

On a roundabout in the middle of a busy crossroads on Ratchadamnoen Klang, the monument was built to commemorate the changeover from absolute to constitutional monarchy on June 24, 1932. It was inaugurated in 1940. Four large granite wings, 24 m high, surround a book representing the constitution.

Thanon Kao San

West of the Democracy Monument, there's a lively street market in Kao San Road, in the area where most of the guest-houses are located. This is one of the best places in the city to buy clothes, CDs, silk and other fabrics, T-shirts and handicrafts.

Ratchadamnoen Stadium

This is one of the main venues for displays of Thai boxing (Muay Thai), with matches held on Mondays, Wednesdays, Thursdays and Sundays. (The other days of the week, fights are held at the Lumphini Stadium on Rama IV Road.)

Modern City

Bangkok's other sights are scattered far and wide. To explore the districts east of the railway line, take the new air-conditioned Skytrain, a fast elevated metro inaugurated in December 1999, or the subway, opened in July 2004 (extensions are under construction). These two systems have done much to alleviate Bangkok's notorious traffic problems.

Wat Benchamabophit

The Marble Temple is just north of the central area, near Dusit Zoo. Rama V was fascinated by Western architecture and retained the services of the Italian architect Hercule Manfredi to build this temple in 1899. The *bot* (chapel) and the cloister were clad in slabs of white marble shipped from Carrara in Italy.

Two marble lions stand at the entrance to the chapel, and 53 bronze statues of Buddha around the cloister illustrate different periods of Buddhist art. The date and place of their origin is inscribed in marble tablets at their feet.

Vimanmek Mansion Museum
This ancient royal summer residence in the grounds of Dusit Palace on Ratchawithi Road is said to be the biggest teak house in the world. The three-storey, 81-roomed palace, built by Rama V at the end of the 19th century, has been restored in its original style, from the reception rooms to the bedchambers. Guided tours in English are available. Traditional dances are performed for visitors in the gardens, a welcome oasis of greenery.

Suan Pakkad Palace
The "Lettuce Garden" Palace at 352 Si Ayutthaya Road, once the property of Prince and Princess Chumbhot, comprises an ensemble of eight traditional teak houses standing in a tropical garden. Apart from a fascinating collection of Asian antiques, includ-

Lion guarding the entrance of Wat Benchamabophit. | **During his lifetime, Jim Thompson's lovely house was the talk of the town.**

ing ceramics, there's a Khon museum displaying masks and costumes of this classical type of theatre.

At the bottom of the garden, the lacquered pavilion from the Ayutthaya period is decorated with gorgeous frescoes in gold leaf on black laquered panels.

Jim Thompson's House
A retired CIA agent, the American Jim Thompson settled permanently in Bangkok after World War II, where he successfully revived Thailand's ailing silk industry. He acquired several traditional canal-side teak houses, joining them into one dwelling, and gathered together a priceless collection of antiques and objets d'art. He disappeared without trace during a journey to Malaysia in 1967. His home at 2 Soi Kasemsan, north of the National Stadium, has been preserved as a museum, displaying very desirable Chinese, Khmer and Thai antiques.

Philatelic Museum
Take the Skytrain to the northern Saphan Kwai (Buffalo Bridge) district and the stamp museum on Pathon Yathon Road. It is signposted from the Sam Sen Nai post office, between Soi 3 and Soi 5; an antique red mailbox stands in front. Here you can see every Thai postage stamp ever issued.

Chatuchak Market
The next stop on the Skytrain line, Mo Chit, is the one for the famous weekend market (open every day but Tuesday). It is huge — just follow the crowds. You'll be captivated by the range of goods on sale: antiques, handicrafts, clothing, odds and ends of all kinds. There are plenty of small restaurants, and activities such as cockfights and battles between carnivorous fish.

Snake Farm
Near the University, along Rama IV Road, the Queen Saovabha Memorial Institute is one of the largest producers of anti-venom serum in Asia. Here you can learn how it is obtained, and — perhaps more useful — what to do if ever you encounter a poisonous snake. There's also a snake pit where you can watch the creatures being fed.

Patpong and Soi Cowboy
Bangkok is famed for its nightlife. As darkness falls and the temperature cools down, people jostle around the stalls of the street traders selling all manner of goods — shirts, handbags, sunglasses, watches, and so on, often at very attractive prices, or snacks such as noodles and a spicy soup. Patpong I and II, south of Rama IV Road, throng with massage parlours, restaurants and bars that

stay open all night long. This is also the night club area, where drinks are exorbitant and young Thai girls in skimpy outfits dance languidly.

The atmosphere is less sordid along Soi Cowboy, a street parallel with Sukhumvit Road (Skytrain stop ASOK), with bars frequented by Thais and expats.

Day Trips
Some of Thailand's most famous sights can be reached easily from Bangkok, with something for all ages and all tastes.

Samut Prakan Crocodile Farm
This "farm" 25 km (15 miles) southeast of Bangkok houses some 60,000 fresh- and seawater crocodiles, as well as snakes, gibbons, lions and elephants, and a small dinosaur museum. Entertainment includes buying chickens to throw to the crocodiles, and watching a man put his head in a crocodile's mouth (performances every hour).

Muang Boran
Further along the same road, the Ancient City is a sort of theme park, laid out in the shape of Thailand and covering 320 acres, with original buildings or models of the country's most important monuments, royal, religious and cultural. You can hire a bicycle to help you get around; it is too big to see on foot. There are also examples of typical Thai houses, and a floating village with several restaurants.

Ko Kret
This small island in the Chao Phraya River, north of the city, is home to a Mon community whose ancestors emigrated from Myanmar more than 30 centuries ago. There are several ancient temples of the Ayutthaya period, but many people come here to see the craftsmen making earthenware pottery, demonstrated at the Ceramics centre. You can also sample traditional Thai desserts, difficult to find elsewhere.

Bang Pa-In
Along the Chao Phraya, about 60 km (37 miles) north of Bangkok, stands the Royal Palace of Bang Pa-In, built in the late 19th and early 20th centuries. It comprises a handsome group of pavilions used by Rama V and Rama VI as their summer residence. The formal gardens are peopled by neoclassical statues; Rama V found the inspiration for the pavilions in Italian baroque and Victorian styles during his travels in Europe. One of the prettiest pavilions, built in 1876, stands in the centre of an artificial pond, reflected in its waters; magnificently carved, it is a jewel of classical Thai architecture,

entitled "the divine seat of personal freedom". Inside is a statue of Rama V.

A tragic event mars the history of this tranquil spot. During an outing on a barge, Sunanda Kumaritana, one of the wives of King Rama V, was drowned along with three of her daughters. It is said that the servants did not dare to jump in and save them as they were forbidden to touch members of the royal family.

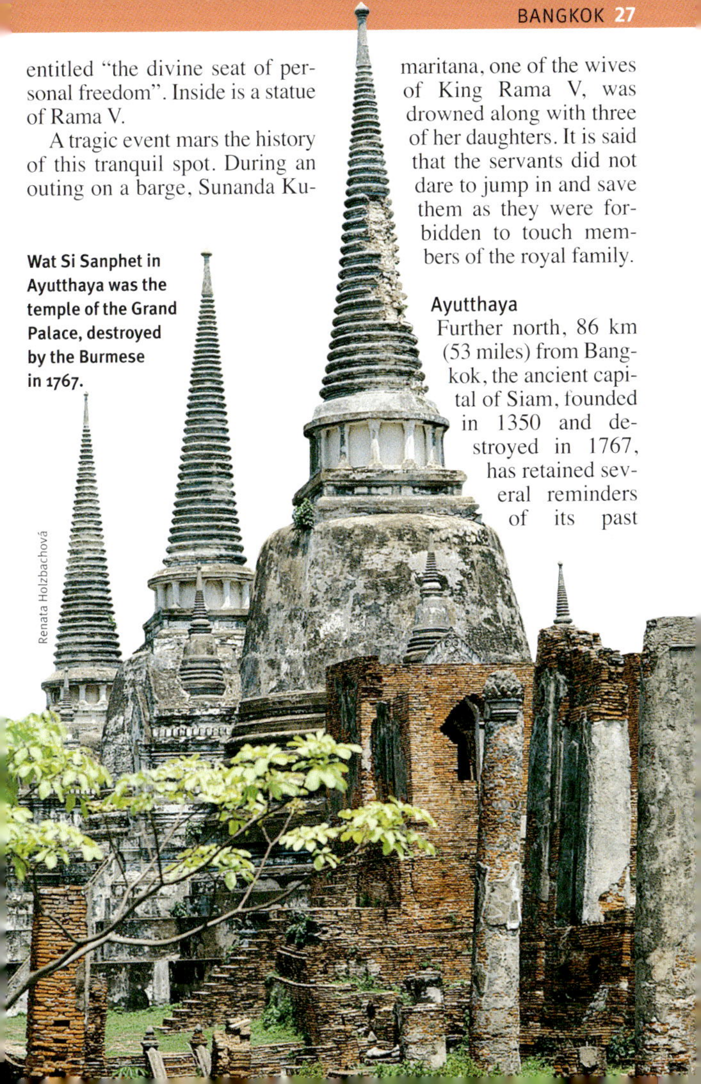

Wat Si Sanphet in Ayutthaya was the temple of the Grand Palace, destroyed by the Burmese in 1767.

Renata Holzbachová

Ayutthaya

Further north, 86 km (53 miles) from Bangkok, the ancient capital of Siam, founded in 1350 and destroyed in 1767, has retained several reminders of its past

splendours. The city was built on an artificial island at the confluence of three rivers, covering an area of 15 sq km (6 sq miles). Altogether, 33 monarchs have reigned here. In the 16th and 17th centuries, Ayutthaya had a million inhabitants. Temples were erected on the island and all around it, on the river banks.

In the centre, **Vihara Phra Mongkol Bophit** was built in the 17th century to house a restored image of Buddha originally sculpted in 1538. Its head had been knocked off when the previous building, a *mandapa* or pillared hall, was struck by lightning. The image was covered with gold leaf in 1990. Nearby, the royal temple of **Wat Phra Sri Sanphet** was the most important in the city, built in 1448 and burned down by the Burmese in order to melt off the gold that covered the Buddha image.

On the other side of Phra Ram park, **Wat Ratchaburana** is easily recognized by its spiral *prang* which escaped destruction. It was built around the tombs of two princes, brothers who killed each other in a battle on elephant-back.

On Rotchana Road, the **Chao Sam Phraya National Museum** displays local artefacts, wooden door panels carved with flowers and religious motifs, 15th-century gold jewellery, and bronze images of Buddha. Relics of Lord Buddha are enshrined in a pavilion. Diagonally opposite, the **Historical Study Centre** is a museum depicting, with the help of models, life as it was in Ayutthaya.

Beside the river, **Chandra Kasem Palace** was built for Prince Naresuan in the 16th century. It was destroyed by the Burmese and lay in ruins until Rama IV ordered its reconstruction; he resided there on his visits to the city. It is now a museum.

You can ride all around the island in a boat to see the many temples. On the mainland, stop off at **Wat Na Phra Men**, where a seated Buddha in stone is considered a work of major importance.

Rose Garden

More than just the rose garden of its name, the private resort of **Suan Sam Phran**, 30 km (18 miles) west of Bangkok stages a **Thai Village Cultural Show**, offering a comprehensive introduction to Thai music, dance and traditional sports. You can also watch skilled craftsmen making umbrellas, pottery and silk cloth.

Sightseeing tours to the Rose Garden generally include a stop at the **Samphran Elephant Ground and Zoo**. Elephant Theme Shows are staged in which the animals dance and play football or perform battle scenes; there is also a crocodile farm with over 10,000 reptiles; some of then engage in wrestling matches.

A wide variety of colourful fruit and vegetables on sale at the floating market of Damnoen Saduak.

Nakhon Pathom

Said to be the oldest town in Thailand, Nakhon Pathom, 60 km (37 miles) west of the capital, features the country's tallest *chedi*: a cone-shaped pagoda 127 m (417 ft) high. It was built in the second half of the 19th century on the site of a temple over 1000 years old. It is claimed that Buddhism was introduced to the country via this town.

Bridge on the River Kwai

The infamous railway bridge spans the river 5 km (3 miles) north of the small town of **Kanchanaburi**, 130 km (80 miles) west of Bangkok. The region is both beautiful and peaceful, but it has not always been so. In 1942 the Japanese occupied Thailand and were planning to conquer all of Asia, including British India. In order to transport troops, supplies and weapons, they had a railway built from Nong Pladuk in Thailand to the town of Thanbyuzayat in Burma (Myanmar), 415 km (258 miles) away. Two-thirds of the line was laid out within the borders of Thailand. Some 61,000 Allied prisoners captured in Malaysia and Singapore, as well as 270,000 Asians, were put to work on the railroad in the most abominable conditions. The death toll was devastating: 12,000 Allied prisoners and over 10,000 Asians lost their lives. The bridge remained in service for 20 months before the Allies bombed it in 1945. Even today, people still find it difficult to forgive the atrocities committed by the Japanese against the Allies: when the Emperor of Japan made an official visit to Great Britain in May 1998, British veterans turned their backs on him as a sign of protest.

Within the enclosure of the temple Wat Chai Chumphon in Kanchanaburi, the **JEATH War Museum** recalls this tragic era. A well-maintained **military cemetery** in Kanchanaburi contains the graves of 6,982 victims.

Damnoen Saduak

The colourful floating markets can no longer be seen in Bangkok itself. Nowadays you have to get up early and travel all the way to the province of **Ratchaburi**, 109 km (68 miles) southwest of the capital, and the Damnoen Saduak *klong*. Throngs of countrywomen in wide-brimmed straw hats paddle their canoes laden with pyramids of exotic fruit and vegetables. Greetings are exchanged, and sales are concluded after an energetic bout of haggling. The canal soon gets jammed with boats, but no one bats an eyelid when they collide. "Mai pen rai"—Not to worry!—is one of the Thais' favourite phrases.

A benign Big Buddha, seated in a Fitness Park near Pattaya.

Gulf of Thailand and Andaman Sea

If you love windsurfing and nightclubs, head straight for the resort of Pattaya, or the quieter Rayong further down the southeast coast. The island of Ko Samet has lovely sandy beaches, while Ko Chang, the country's second-largest island, after Phuket, is the ideal hideaway.

On the southwest coast of the Gulf of Thailand, the closest resorts to the capital are Cha Am and Hua Hin. With 2,710 km (1,683 miles) of coastline, the Thai peninsula unfurls a carpet of coconut palms, rubber trees and white sand, with strings of paradise islands in the Gulf of Thailand and in the Andaman Sea, where Phuket is the jewel in the country's crown.

Southeast Coast

The coast stretches for 500 km (310 miles) down to the Cambodian border. Its most popular resort is Pattaya, a 2-hour drive from Bangkok. But the accent here is on fun and nightlife. If you're looking for unspoiled beaches and clean waters for swimming, an outlying coral island will be more to your taste.

Pattaya

Up to 1959 this was just a small fishing village on a beautiful stretch of sand. Then American troops adopted it as a base for R&R — rest and relaxation — during the Vietnam War. Hotels, bungalows, condominiums and restaurants flourished; now up to 4 million visitors come every year. The seafront is a succession of shopping malls, fashion boutiques, restaurants, bars, nightclubs, discos, massage parlours and tourist accommodation; the lovely beach is but a distant memory. One of the highlights of Pattaya is the food — whether you choose five-star restaurants or waterfront eateries, the seafood is first-rate and the variety limitless.

To get around, there are plenty of collective taxis which will put you down wherever you like for a very modest fare. Otherwise, if you want more freedom, hire a motorbike. To find out what's on, seek out a copy of *Pattaya Mail*, an English-language weekly that lists all local activities. There's no time to get bored: you can practise all kinds of sport from horse riding to golf, and shop till you drop in every kind of outlet from market stall to shopping mall.

The third floor of the Royal Garden Plaza is devoted entirely to entertainment, with 3D show, cinemas, video games, and a **Ripley's Believe It or Not Museum** (or "odditorium") displaying over 300 weird and wonderful objects collected around the world, together with puzzles, optical illusions, and scales that tell you your weight on the moon. Next door is the **Haunted Adventure**.

Hat Naklua

A 10-minute drive to the north of Pattaya, Hat Naklua has retained its fishing-village atmosphere despite the onslaught of highrise hotels.

Set on a rocky promontory, the **Sanctuary of Truth** (Prasat Sut Ja-Tum) is a project undertaken in 1981 to build a four-wing temple illustrating the four major architectural influences seen in Thailand: Hindu, Khmer, Chinese and Thai. It was the brainchild of Khun Lek, the multi-millionaire who also created the Ancient City near Bangkok. A team of 250 woodcarvers can be seen working at any one time. When finished, the complex will include smaller buildings and guesthouses. At present you can observe work in progress; a guide will show you around.

Hat Jomtien

Southwards, Pattaya continues round Jomtien Bay, 6 km (4 miles) long and popular with families. All manner of watersports are practised at here in the clear waters of the bay. Between Pattaya and Jomtien, on a high promontory reached via Pattaya Hill Road, is a huge seated Buddha, flanked by a Hindu Buddha and seven small images, one for every day of the week.

For views from even higher, go to the **Pattaya Park Beach Resort**, which has revolving restaurants on the 52nd and 53rd floors of its tower, and observation decks on the 54th and 55th floors.

Mini Siam

Excursions are organized to this park that displays several fine Thai temples in miniature, but also Cambodia's Angkor Wat, the Sydney Opera House, the Eiffel Tower and Arc de Triomphe from Paris, Egypt's Valley of the Kings and Abu Simbel, London's Tower Bridge, Germany's Neuschwanstein Castle, and other famous monuments.

Nong Nooch Village

This inland resort, 15 km (9 miles) to the east, is the site of cultural shows with displays of dance, music, Thai boxing and other martial arts, cock fighting and so on. There is also an elephant show, a tropical garden with many species of orchid, and cactus and bonsai collections.

Ko Larn (Ko Lan)

To get to Coral Island out in the middle of Pattaya Bay, you can take the cheap but slow public ferry, which will deposit you at the town (you will then have to take a taxi to get to a beach), a speedboat from Pattaya Beach, or an organized day trip which will include a trip on a glass-bottomed boat to see the coral gardens. Scuba expeditions enable you to explore a couple of wrecks near Sattahip. The half-dozen beaches are lined with souvenir stalls selling beachwear and handicrafts, and there are plenty of food stalls and restaurants.

Rayong
This fishing village further south along the coast is developing as a resort but is as yet unspoiled. The beaches are as close to perfect as you could imagine.

Ko Samet
Young Thais love to spend a day on this little island off the coast near Rayong—and for good reason. You'll find coconut palms, the sea, white sand and bungalow accommodation. There are nowhere near as many tourists as in Pattaya. As the island is part of a national park, it is still protected (though who knows for how long) from inappropriate development. To reach the island, there is a shuttle from the village of Ban Phe.

Ko Chang
This island is the ideal place for those who want to avoid crowds and a hectic nightlife. There are no towns, hardly any roads, and the rainforest, which covers 70 per cent of the island, comes right down to the edge of the white sand beaches. Watersports and inland tours are arranged by the resorts

Thai Peninsula
Altogether, the coasts of the Thai Peninsula stretch over 2,710 km (1,683 miles), an expanse of white sand shaded by coconut palms and rubber trees, with constellations of islands in the Gulf of Thailand to the east—the Sunrise Coast—and the Andaman Sea to the west. A dozen national marine parks have been created to preserve the environment.

Many Thais have left their homes to settle in one of the 14 southern provinces which produce the nation's most important exports: coconut, tin and rubber. The further south you go, the more you will notice changes in the landscape. Rice paddies give way to rubber tree plantations, Malay is spoken as much as Thai, and the domes of mosques rise above the trees.

Cha Am
This resort, 210 km (130 miles) south of Bangkok, was created in the 1960s. Its beautiful beaches are shaded by slender, feathery casuarina trees, and the seafront hotels bathed in morning sun-

shine. Cha Am has everything to make a stay unforgettable—a lovely, quiet beach and calm seas suitable for swimming. Near the station, there's a traditional market; you can also visit a **reptile park** and two monasteries, **Wat Sai Yoi** and **Wat Nong Chaeng**.

Within the grounds of a military camp on Bang Kra beach, about 10 km (6 miles) south of Cha Am, **Mrigadayavan Palace** was a summer residence built by King Rama VI in 1924. The architecture of this Palace of Love and Hope is known as Thai-Victorian style, with 16 buildings of golden teak linked by elevated covered walkways open on both sides to catch the breeze. They comprise an audience hall, the men's and ladies' quarters, and two beach pavilions. At the back of the palace are the more modest servants' quarters. The palace is open every day except Wednesday, and no shorts, short skirts or sleeveless T-shirts are allowed. In the grounds you can follow a nature trail on wooden walkways through a mangrove swamp, where there is a tower for bird-watching.

Colourful fishing boats at anchor in Pattaya harbour. | There's something deliciously quaint about Hua Hin's railway station. | Three-wheeled transport in Petchaburi.

Hua Hin

The longest-established resort on this coast, Hua Hin lies 20 km (12 miles) south of Cha Am. It was launched in 1910 when Prince Chakrabongse, brother of Rama VI, built a luxurious hunting lodge to accommodate and entertain his guests. It soon became a summer retreat for the entire court, and when the railway was completed in the early 1920s wealthy Thais used to come in their droves. In 1926 Rama VII had his new summer residence, **Klai Klangwan** ("Far from Worries") built, and he was here in 1932 when he heard the news that the monarchy had been abolished. Today, the royal family occasionally stays at the palace, as you may suspect when you see naval ships patrolling out to sea.

The best way to arrive here is by train, arriving at the old-fashioned station; note the palatial red and white teak building formerly reserved for VIPs. The prestigious Orient Express to Singapore always makes a stop here. Though the town has plenty of modern hotels, banks and shiny new office buildings, you will still come across relics of a bygone era. The charming **Railway Hotel**, built in the 1920s by the state railway company, was renovated in the 1980s and has retrieved its original teak and marble splendour. It now forms a wing of the Sofitel resort, surrounded by vast gardens dotted with topiary animals, its swimming pool overlooking the shore. Even if you don't stay there, you can sip tea and sample delicious pastries in The Museum, the hotel's comfortable café. Next to the Hilton Hotel is another good café, World News, which has lots of international newspapers on hand.

For some local colour, look around **Chatchai market** in the town centre; its stalls of dried fish, giant prawns, fruit, flowers and spices are irresistible. At dusk, the **Night Market** on Dechanuchit Road takes over; the food prepared at the open-air stalls can be exquisite (watch out for pickpockets.)

If you're in need of calm, visit **Wat Ampharam**, decorated with interesting wall paintings illustrating the life of Buddha.

Less frequented by tourists than Phuket or Pattaya and popular with the Thais, the beach stretches for more than 5 km (3 miles). Hua Hin is famed for its 18-hole golf course overlooking the sea. It is overlooked by a large rock guarding the bay and which gave Hua Hin its name, "Stone Head".

Kaeng Krachan National Park

Between Petchaburi and Cha Am, on the border with Myanmar, this is the largest national park in

Thailand. It was established in 1981 and covers almost 3,000 sq km (1,100 sq miles). The Tenasserim mountain range cuts through it, and the landscape is stunning, with torrents and waterfalls in the evergreen forest. Among the animals are leopard, tiger, elephant, gaur, gibbons and over 250 species of bird.

Khao Sam Roi Yot National Park

South of Hua Hin, this was Thailand's first coastal park, created in 1996. It covers 98 sq km (39 sq miles); the name means the Mountain with Three Hundred Peaks. The landscape includes wooded mountains, freshwater marsh and coastal habitats, with mangroves, sandy beaches, caves and offshore islands. Among the wildlife are three species of primate: spectacled langur, crab-eating macaque and the slow lorris. There are also goat antelope, pangolin, porcupine and mongoose, while dolphins are sometimes sighted off shore. More than 300 species of bird have been spotted, over half of which are migratory.

Climb up the steep trail to the top of **Khao Daeng**, alt. 157 m (515 ft) for a panoramic view over the coast and mountains. From **Laem Sala Beach** you can follow a trail to **Phraya Nakhon** cave, made of two sinkholes with trees growing inside.

Surat Thani

Some 500 km (300 miles) south of Bangkok, Surat Thani is the gateway to some of Thailand's best beaches and paradise islands: ferries leave from here for Ko Samui. There's little to see in the town, which is a commercial centre and port dealing in rubber and coconuts.

Ko Samui

Thailand's third-largest island, with an area of 250 sq km (96 sq miles), is surrounded by a host of islets. For Europeans in search of the exotic, it was a dream destination in the 1970s, but now it has become overcrowded, especially since the construction of an airport and the creation of regular ferry links with four ports on the mainland.

The first settlers were Chinese farmers and fishermen who arrived two centuries ago. Today, the 40,000 inhabitants, mostly of Chinese or Malay origin, derive their income from the tourist industry, but also from the cultivation of coconut palms.

The ferry deposits visitors in the small town of **Na Thon**. From the landing, minibuses operate a shuttle service. The first beautiful beach to the north is **Ban Thai**. If you're looking for somewhere quiet, consider **Bang Baw Bay**, usually deserted because of the rocks exposed at low tide. To the east,

Mae Nam beach is fairly peaceful and has not been spoiled by tourist development. **Bo Phut** is even quieter. The nearby village is small and picturesque, with several teak houses and painted boats. It is one of the oldest settlements on Ko Samui.

On the east side of the island is **Chaweng**. People who came here in the 1980s still think of it with nostalgia, for it used to be a blissful stretch of white sand with a sprinkling of bungalows. Now it is one of the most crowded beaches on the island, the environment has changed beyond recognition, and the clientele, too. Offshore is the tiny island of **Mat Lang**. Also on the east coast, **Lamai** is another popular resort.

Ang Thong National Marine Park

A popular day trip from Ko Samui, the park covers an archipelago of 42 islands. The geology is one of soaring walls of rugged limestone and fascinating rock formations caused by erosion. **Mae Ko** island has one of the loveliest of all the many lovely beaches, as well as an emerald saltwater lake, Thale Nai, while **Sam Sao** is known for its huge arch of rock and the coral reef. In the tropical rainforest you may see langurs (long-tailed monkeys) while the coast is home to reef egrets, sea eagles, hairy-nosed otters and turtles.

Ko Pha Ngan

North of Ko Samui, only 15 km (9 miles) away (less than an hour by boat), Pha Ngan is smaller, much more rustic, and its roads are mere tracks. Because it has not been overdeveloped, it still has an authentic atmosphere and has become a magnet for backpackers. The island is wooded and hilly, and has several waterfalls. The coast is frilled with superb beaches and coves. **Hat Yuan** in the southwest is one of the prettiest, though the waves can be strong. Near the small village of Ban Tai, you can visit a cave temple, **Wat Khao Tham**.

But Pha Ngan is mainly known for its groovy **Full Moon parties** held once a month on the crescent-shaped beach of **Hat Rin**. Up to 10,000 people gather here to dance from dusk till well after dawn, encouraged by local and international DJs. Jugglers and fire-eaters entertain the crowds.

Ko Tao

About 6 hours by boat from Surat Thani, this small island is a favourite with divers, whether beginners or experienced. Diving schools offer training at all levels, and the underwater scenery is unrivalled. Only 21 sq km (8 sq miles) in area, the island is mountainous and its beaches are sheltered from the wind. The boat lands at **Ban Mae Hat**, an unspoiled

All of Thailand in one image: tropical fruit, intense colours and a friendly smile.

Renata Holzbachová

village with stilt houses and bamboo huts.

If a fisherman offers you a trip to **Nang Yuan Island**, then seize the chance. In a few minutes you'll reach a true natural wonder: three small wooded hills where a few bungalows nestle, linked by causeways of fine sand, three superb beaches and a couple of restaurants looking out over the sea.

Nakhon Si Thammarat

From the 8th to the 13th centuries, Nakhon Si Thammarat, some 800 km (500 miles) south of the capital, was part of the Srivijaya civilization. At that time, this southern area was under the influence of Sumatra, and the province did not form part of Thailand until Bangkok was founded. Proud of its ancient heritage, Nakhon Si Thammarat is considered to be the birthplace of shadow puppet theatre and of classical dance *(lakhon)*. Marionettes of buffalo-hide and dance masks are still made here.

Wat Mahathat, one of the oldest temples in Thailand (AD 757), is also the biggest in the southern part of the country. The upper part of its *chedi*, 77 m (252 ft) high, is topped with a gold spire said to weigh between 600 and 1000 kg. It was built in the 13th century to house relics of the Buddha brought from Sri Lanka.

Nearby on **Si Thammasok**, you can visit a shadow puppet workshop to see a master craftsman cutting out the designs on lacquered hides.

The **National Museum** displays many religious objects and artefacts from the Dvaravati and Ayutthaya periods. There is a fine 5th-century statue of Vishnu, the oldest in South East Asia, and two rare Dong Song bronze drums.

Krabi

On the west side of the peninsula, Krabi is capital of the region of the same name, featuring rubber tree plantations and mangrove swamps. Fossilized shells, more than 60 million years old, are found along the coast.

The beaches, below steep cliffs, are idyllic. **Hat Nang** is tucked into a bay, but there are others, even more spectacular, stretching around **Phang Nga** bay. **Hat Re Lai** is surrounded by towering rocks and tapers off into a coral reef.

Khao Phanom Bencha National Park culminates at 1,397 m (4,583 ft), providing a watershed for Krabi province. It incorporates 80 coastal isles and is largely moist evergreen forest. The fauna includes wild pigs, panthers, black bears, mouse deer, langurs, gibbons and hornbills. A few hundred metres from the park headquarters, **Huai To** waterfall is 70 to 80 m (230–262 ft) high and cascades over 11 levels into a clear pool. A 2-km hike from the headquarters, **Khao Phueng** cave has spectacular stalactites and stalagmites in intricate formations.

Other caves burrow into the limestone hills around town. Some of them shelter the shrines of **Wat Tham Sua**. Above **Tham Phra Nang** beach, there's a cave dedicated to a legendary princess. Fishermen leave offerings here before setting out to sea.

Ko Phi Phi

These two remote islands, designated a national park, can be reached in two hours by boat from Krabi. The trip takes you past beautiful beaches scattered with bungalows looking out over the sea.

Ko Phi Phi Don is the larger of the two islands; it has all the elements of a treasure isle with white sand beaches fringed by swaying palms, little creeks, turquoise sea, coral gardens, bungalows by the shore—and excellent restaurants. Spoil yourself and rent a bamboo hut by the sea. Lazing in your hammock, you'll hear nothing but the gentle surge of the waves and the whisper of the breeze. Now and then, you can bestir yourself for a swim in the sea, among the colourful fish and blue starfish.

Boat trips are organized to the other island, **Ko Phi Phi Le**, from the little port of Ton Sai. The scenery of towering limestone cliffs is breathtaking. The boats generally stop at the so-called "Viking Caves" where sea gypsies *(Chao Lay)*, the descendants of sea-faring nomads, clamber up rickety bamboo scaffolding to collect the swallows' nests built up to 100 m (300 ft) high. They are the main ingredient in birds' nest soup.

Further on, **Maya Bay** comes into view, in its setting of wooded cliffs. This is where *The Beach*, with Leonardo DiCaprio, was filmed. The emerald-green water is so clear you can see all the wonders of the sea bed. Building on Phi Phi Le is forbidden.

Ko Lanta

Further down the coast, Ko Lanta, with 20,000 inhabitants, is partly owned by sea gypsies, while the rest is protected as a national marine park. Tree felling is severely restricted, and new buildings are made of natural materials and blend into the surroundings. The traditional economy of fishing, prawn farming and the cultivation of coconut, rice, fruit and rubber has been supplemented by the increase of tourism in recent years; there are now some 60 resorts, most of them family-run. The 20 km (12 miles) of beaches are all west-facing, so it has become a tradition to take drinks while the sun sets behind the horizon. Needless to say, the snorkelling is superb.

Phang Nga and its Bay

The town of Phang Nga is 95 km (59 miles) north of Krabi. Within the confines of **Wat Phraphat Prachimkhet** is a cave, Phung Chang (Elephant Belly) with stalagmites and stalactites, and a stream that flows all year round.

The town overlooks a bay, **Ao Phang Nga**, a national marine park with an area of 40,000 sq km (16,000 sq miles) comprising more than 40 islands clad in vegetation and eroded into weird shapes. The scenery is similar to that of Guilin in southern China or Vietnam's famous Ha Long Bay, with limestone rocks rising out of the water to heights of up to 300 m (1,000 ft). Kingfishers and eagles flock to this area where the sea is very shallow.

Excursions are arranged from Krabi or Phuket. You can tour the bay by motorboat or canoe, the best way of getting close to the little islands honeycombed with caves and through tunnels hollowed out by the tides. Among the most popular is **Tham Lot**, a wide limestone cave with stalactites. **Khao Phingkan** is made up of two hilly islets, one of which is split into two parts, leaning one against the other. Together with mushroom-like **Ko Tapu**, a few hundred metres away, the scenery will seem familiar—this was the backdrop to James Bond's adventures in *The Man with the Golden Gun*. **Khao Khian** (Writing Hill) island has cave paintings of unknown origin, estimated to be

---

The most beautiful islands
Phuket for the high standard of its hotels and its fine sand; **Ko Phi Phi** for boat excursions through the caves; **Ko Samui** for the variety of its beaches and their convivial atmosphere.

3,000 years old, depicting human figures, crocodiles, dolphins and sharks.

Ko Panyi is the only Muslim island in the country; its white mosque can be seen from a distance. Fishermen from Malaysia to the south landed here and settled over a century ago. In the village, more than 500 houses and the school are built on stilts over the sea. The economy depends on tourism, fish-farming and the sale of shells, and as space is at a premium, concrete piles have been driven in for more buildings. Ko Panyi is a popular place for a seafood lunch; there are several restaurants and a modest guesthouse with a few basic rooms.

Among other islands worth exploring in the bay, **Ko Hong**, with several caves accessible only by canoe, has a lagoon on the west shore and a white sand beach in a bay on the east side. **Ko Phanak** has an emerald lagoon which can be accessed only by a narrow opening at low tide, while the two islets of **Ko Khai** boast translucent waters, powdery sand and tranquillity.

Phuket

With an area of 550 sq km (212 sq miles), Thailand's biggest island is linked to the mainland by the Sarasin Bridge, a journey of 885 km (550 miles) from Bangkok.

The first inhabitants of Phuket were sea gypsies; their descendants still live in a couple of fishing villages. The island's rich tin deposits were first exploited in the 16th century, and Chinese immigrants were brought in to work the mines. Tin remained the major source of wealth until the 1980s, but now tourism and the production of rubber, from trees planted at the beginning of the 20th century, are the mainstays. The 260,000 inhabitants enjoy the highest standard of living in the whole country.

The best of the famous white-sand beaches are on the west coast, facing the often dramatic sunsets. The rapid growth of tourism since the 1960s brought a rash of development at the main resorts, especially Patong. But tranquil spots are not difficult to find. Water sports are the main attraction, and for variation there's golf or tennis, or boat trips around the islands of Ao Phang Nga. For a trip around the island, you can join an organized tour or rent a car or jeep, a three-wheeled *samlor* or *tuk-tuk*, or take the bus (the station is near the market on Ranong Road).

Phuket Town

Most of Phuket Town (population 80,000) was built from the mid-19th century onwards and is modern concrete, but there are still some attractive two-storey houses in the Sino-Portuguese style, introduced in the 16th century. The ground floors are arcaded, and the façades, window frames and pillars adorned with stucco decoration. Many of these buildings in the Thalang Road area have been restored. For a good view over the district, go up Khan Rang (Phuket Hill) on the northern edge of town.

Ranong Road is the site of the daily market, open from early morning till late afternoon. Here you can feast your eyes on the colourful mounds of fruit, vegetables, spices and exotic flowers. Everything is sold here from household goods to shrimp paste.

A short walk from the market, **Put Jaw**, the oldest Chinese temple in Phuket, is dedicated to Kuan Yin, the Goddess of Mercy. In the middle hall there's an image of the goddess and several rudimentary fortune-telling devices. You are expected to leave a donation, intended for the upkeep of the temple.

Next door, elaborate **Jui Tui** shrine with carved entrance doors and dragons on the roof is dedicated to a vegetarian god, Kiu Wong In. His red-faced image

Dragons form the balustrades at Wat Chalong. | You'll have no problem finding a beach all to yourself.

stands on the altar; the colour denotes benevolence. Phuket celebrates a Vegetarian Festival every year during the ninth month of the Chinese calendar, which is based on the phases of the moon.

Just off Krabi Road, **Sanjao Sam San** temple is dedicated to the Goddess of the Sea. The entrance is flanked by two lions. New boats are brought here to be blessed.

Wat Chalong

Southwest of town, this is the island's biggest Buddhist temple. Two stone elephants stand guard at the entrance; inside are several images of Buddha covered in gold leaf. The temple is associated with two monks, Luang Pho Chaem and Luang Pho Chuang, who were renowned for their knowledge of herbal medicines and who took care of the injured during the violent tin miners' rebellion of 1876. They acted as mediators in the dispute, finally achieving an agreement. Statues of the monks stand in the sermon hall *(viharn)*. People come here for blessings and to receive a good luck charm, consisting of a string tied around the wrist.

Ra Wai

Continuing south from Wat Chalong, you reach the coast. In the south of the island, Ra Wai is famous for its shells, revealed at low tide. Many beautiful specimens are displayed at the Sea Shell Museum.

Promthep Cape

The southernmost point of the island has a lighthouse with viewing platform overlooking Nai Harn beach, the most spectacular place to watch the setting sun.

Thalang

About half way between Phuket Town and the airport, Thalang is the island's former capital, now a pleasant village. At an intersection to the south, the **Heroines' Memorial** honours the sisters Muk and Chan who successfully defended Thalang against an attack from the Burmese in 1786. They disguised 500 women and girls as soldiers, gave them sticks shaped like weapons and drilled them in full view of the attackers. It was a success: after a month's siege, the invaders withdrew.

Wat Phra Thong

Just north of Thalang, this temple houses a half-buried golden Buddha, coated with plaster by the villagers to avoid it attracting the Burmese. The legend goes that a local boy tethered his water buffalo to a shaft sticking out of the ground. Soon afterwards he fell ill and died; his father had a dream telling him to go to the shaft and unearth it. He attempted

Soak up the sun one one of the beaches along Phuket's coast.

to do so, and discovered that it was the tip of a big statue of Buddha. It was too large to dig out, so he built a temple around it. Along the walls of the temple are seven more Buddha images, all in a different posture, one for every day of the week, and covered in gold leaf. Each one has a donation box with a label indicating its good effects (wealth, good health, and so on).

Ton Sai Waterfall Forest Park
East of Thalang, a picturesque waterfall cascades down limestone slopes, forming pools ideal for bathing. There's a small restaurant at the headquarters.

Khao Phra Thaeo National Park
East again, this wildlife conservation centre covers a large expanse of creeper-clad virgin forest, including the rare Governor's or White Back palm. Among the wildlife are langurs, gibbons, macaques, mouse deer, barking deer, porcupines and lizards, as well as many species of bird.

Beaches
On Phuket, every little bay has its own character and charm. Gently sloping stretches of white sand, separated by rocky headlands, make up most of the west coast.

Beginning in the north, **Mai Khao** near the airport is one of the longest and least accessible—fortunately for the turtles who come ashore to lay their eggs.

Nai Yang, part of a national park, is almost as quiet, and usually has clear water for snorkelling. Just south is the peaceful **Nai Thon**.

At **Pansea** on the central coast, Phuket's most exclusive resorts are hidden away among the trees.

Against a backdrop of coconut palms, **Surin** is fairly quiet and not yet over-developed, unlike **Patong**, further south, the island's most popular beach. Its great crescent of superb sand, covered with row upon row of beach chairs, is paralleled by Beach Road, packed from one end to the other with a succession of hotels, shopping malls, restaurants, bars, massage parlours and discos. By night it's thronged with strolling tourists, mingling with a variety of vendors, fortune tellers, tricksters and transvestites. For something much more secluded, head for picturesque **Laem Sing**, at the bottom of a path.

The development is creeping relentlessly southwards towards lovely **Karon** and **Kata**, the last beaches on the west coast before **Nai Harn** and its yacht club.

Khao Lak
An hour's drive north of Phuket, Khao Lak is a scenic resort on the threshold of a national park of untouched jungle, rebuilt since the tsunami of December 2004.

A carved lintel of the central tower at Surin shrine represents figures of Hindu mythology.

The Centre

East of the main routes leading to the Golden Triangle in the far north, the central part of Thailand occupies a plateau where dry and rainy seasons are equally hard on the land. Though the area is infertile, and off the beaten tourist track, it is rich in history. The most interesting Khmer temples outside Cambodia can be found here.

The road north takes you through the Mae Nam plain, where paddy fields stretch as far as the eye can see. Dotted among them are the silhouettes of stooping women, thinning out and replanting the green shoots, their faces hidden beneath straw hats.

Khmer Temples

The largest town in the region is **Nakhon Ratchasima** (or Khorat), a former US base 220 km (137 miles) northeast of Bangkok. To visit Phimai and the temples, you can hire a car or motorbike, or take the local bus.

Phimai

This historic site lies 45 km (28 miles) east of Nakhon Ratchasima; there are several inns offering unpretentious if adequate accommodation. The ancient Khmer city, founded in the 12th century, was linked directly to Angkor by road. It was built on the same precise and symbolic plan as the Angkor temples, with water-filled moats representing the cosmic ocean, towers *(prang)* symbolizing the sacred mountains, and a central, dominant tower standing for Mount Meru, home of the Hindu gods.

Prasat Phanom Rung

Near the border with Cambodia, this is the most spectacular Khmer monument in Thailand. It lies 132 km (82 miles) east of Nakhon Ratchasima, past Nang Rong; 50 km (30 miles) south of Buri Ram if you are coming from Phimai. The shrine was built on a mountain, on the ridge of an extinct volcano, in the early 12th century at the beginning of the Angkor Wat period. The temple dedicated to the Hindu god Shiva has been well restored and has much charm. An imposing avenue, 160 m (175 yd) long, sweeps up to a monumental staircase guarded by large *nagas* (aquatic divinities). Inside the temple, the carved lintels and pediments are superb.

Surin

East of Buri Ram, Surin, most of the year a sleepy town, is known for its annual **Elephant Round-up Festival** which takes place during the second or third weekend of November. Some 150 animals take part in the pageants and parades, and shows are staged to demonstrate their skill at work and in ancient warfare, as well as their behaviour in their natural habitat.

Do not miss **Prasat Si Khoraphum**, a shrine built in the 12th century. The tallest of its five brick *prang* is decorated with superb sculptures representing scenes from Hindu mythology.

Wat Prathat Phanom

In the far northeast of Thailand, on the border with Laos and only 1 km from the Mekong river, this temple complex is one of the twelve pilgrimage centres corresponding to the twelve-year animal cycle (it represents year 9, associated with the monkey). It is believed that the Buddha himself visited here, accompanied by his disciple Ananda. Built on Phu Kamphra, a sacred hill, the temple is in the elegant Laotian style of the 15th–16th centuries, with a central *that* (or *chedi*) 57 m (187 ft) tall, clad with 110 kg gold. The *chedi* collapsed during heavy rains in 1975; after rebuilding, it was inaugurated by King Bhumibol four years later. Pilgrims come here to make wishes: they buy a bird in a bamboo cage, walk round the temple praying before images of the Buddha and ancient spirit stones, then release the birds in the hope that they will carry their wishes to the heavens. An annual seven-day festival is held in late January or early February, when the greatest numbers of pilgrims gather at the shrine.

Sukhothai

Located 466 km (290 miles) north of Bangkok, the city, whose name means "Dawn of Happiness", was captured from the Khmers and became capital of the first kingdom of Siam from 1238 to 1376, The old city has been listed as a UNESCO World Heritage Site since 1994. In the modern town, 20 minutes away from the historic centre, there are several hotels and inns providing comfortable accommodation.

Until the reign of Rama Khamhaeng (1277–1317), art forms had been influenced by the Indian and Khmer civilizations. The king invented the Thai script, heralding a veritable blossoming of art and architecture in a specific Thai style. Monumental statuary was developed, reaching its zenith after 1350. Architects attempted a new technique of construction using bricks supported on foundations of pillars, while at the same time, sculptors considerably enhanced the decoration of Buddha images.

Historic Park

Pleasantly landscaped with plenty of greenery, the site is open daily. Of the twenty temples within the old city walls, a dozen have been restored. The biggest and most important is **Wat Mahathat**, originally surrounded by a moat. In the centre is a *chedi* in the lotus-bud shape, with four Khmer-style *prang* around it.

At **Wat Sa Si**, you can see a great seated Buddha surrounded by columns, mirrored in a reflecting pond with huge lotus flowers floating on the surface.

The **Ramkhamhaeng National Museum**, also in the park, displays a large collection of Buddha statues and ceramics found on the site. Particularly noteworthy is a statue of a Walking Buddha, a posture in the unique Sukhothai style, depicting the Buddha descending from a higher plane of existence.

Buddha in reflection in Sukhothai's historic park.

Wat Si Chum

North of the historic site, Wat Si Chum boasts an imposing seated Buddha 15 m (50 ft) high, made of brick covered with stucco and filling the entire building. In the wall of the *mondop* (square hall) behind the statue is a hidden staircase leading to a space behind the head. The king would climb up here and address the worshippers, pretending to be the voice of Buddha. The stairway vault (no longer open to the public) is studded with engraved panels illustrating episodes from the *jatakas*, stories of the previous incarnations of Buddha.

Phitsanulok

Southeast of Sukhothai, this town is frequented by the many pilgrims who come to **Wat Phra Si**. The temple contains one of the country's most revered statues—the gilded bronze Chinnarat Buddha in the posture described as "subduing evil".

Tak

Southwest of Sukhothai, the capital of Tak province was once a prosperous river port for merchandise shipped between Bangkok and Chiang Mai. The land is wooded, mountainous and rich in game, and the vegetation lush with rubber plantations, banana trees and frangipanis.

Bhumibol Dam

Some 60 km (40 miles) north of Tak city, the dam is built on the Mae Ping River. It forms a long, meandering lake that stretches northwards up to Chiang Mai.

Doi Suthep temple at Chiang Mai is a major pilgrimage site.

The North

In the foothills of the northern mountains, the provincial capital of Chiang Mai lies more than 700 km (400 miles) from Bangkok. Until as recently as 1920, when the railway was built, it was only accessible by river or on elephant back. Even today the route offers plenty to discover.

Further north, Chiang Rai is at the heart of the so-called Golden Triangle, the region where the borders of Laos, Myanmar and Thailand come together. It is dotted with small villages where you can meet tribes such as the Padaung or the Shan.

Lampang

In this attractive town, some 100 km (60 miles) south of Chiang Mai, people still travel around in horse-drawn carriages. The main temple is **Wat Phra Keo Don Tao**; it housed the famous Emerald Buddha until 1468 and has elaborate decoration. Several other delightful temples recall the ancient kingdom of Lan Na and reveal a Burmese influence. **Wat Pongsanuk Tai** is rather unusual, with its *mondop* covered by a three-storey roof; **Wat Seng Muang Ma** contains superb painted wooden panels; while **Wat Pratu Pong** is simply exquisite.

Near Lampang, you should not miss **Wat Phra That Lampang Luang**—a veritable citadel or *wiang*—built in the 11th century.

Lamphun

Now a peaceful and rather sleepy little town, Lamphun was the capital of the ancient Mon kingdom of Haripunchai, founded by Queen Chamadevi when she was attempting to escape from Khmer troops. Overlooking the River Ping, **Wat Phra That Haripunchai** was built in 1044 on the site of a former palace made of wood. The striking *chedi* is 46 m (151 ft) high and covered in gold. It was built in 1467 in the Lan Na style.

Chiang Mai

The "Rose of the North" or the "City of Flowers" is still elegant, with ancient ramparts and moats protecting its centre of teak houses, despite the fact that it has grown into a modern town with 185,000 inhabitants. Its very remoteness long preserved it from the influence of the outside world.

Founded by King Mengrai at the end of the 13th century, Chiang Mai became the religious and cultural capital of the kingdom of Lan Na, reaching its zenith during the reign of Tilokaraja (1442–87). Enemy armies, both Mon and Khmer, attempted to invade the city, but they could never break through the sturdy defences, a square rampart built by 100,000 men. Chiang Mai's long-standing supremacy was ended in 1588 when it was taken by the Burmese under the king of Pegu. It was not until 1775 that Taksin, king of Thonburi, took back the great northern city. But it was fully integrated into Thailand only in 1939, when it was made provincial capital.

Here more than elsewhere in Thailand, the craft industry is thriving, especially lacquerware, fabrics and parasols. The townsfolk are renowned for their kindness and hospitality, and the women for their beauty. The mountains provide a superb backdrop to the town, and all the temples are within cycling distance. They have teak decoration as in Myanmar, sometimes gilded.

Wat Chiang Man

While the city was undergoing construction, King Mengrai lived in this temple on Ratchaphanikai Road. It is Chiang Mai's oldest, built in 1297, and contains remarkable woodcarvings, as well as 15 statues of elephants supporting the *chedi*. In the large *viharn* stands the oldest Buddha in Chiang Mai, holding a begging bowl and dated 1465. Two other images of Buddha, kept in the smaller *viharn*, are particularly venerated. The crystal Pra Setang Khamani belonged to the wife of Mengrai and is said to protect against disaster. The 8th-century Pra Sila, or Marble Buddha, is a bas-relief from Sri Lanka, depicting the Buddha overcoming the elephant Nalagiri. It is thought to have the power to bring rain.

Wat Phra Singh

In the north of town, the Temple of the Lion Buddha is without doubt the most interesting. Its library is superbly decorated. The statue of Buddha, originally from Sri Lanka, dates from the 14th century. The head was stolen in 1922 and replaced by a replica.

> **Songkran.** In Chiang Mai, the Thai New Year or Songkran is also known as the "water festival", because everyone splashes everyone else with water from the town moat. It is celebrated in April, when the sun moves into Aries. Beauty contests succeed processions, shows and other events, held over several days. For a few bahts, you can buy a caged bird and set it free.

Renata Holzbachová

Wat Chedi Luang
The ruins of this imposing *chedi* stand fairly close to Wat Phra Singh. The pagoda, 500 years old, was damaged during the earthquake that shook the town in 1545. The well-travelled Emerald Buddha, now at Wat Phra Kaeo in Bangkok, was kept in this temple for 84 years.

Wat Suan Dok
Outside the town walls on the Suthep road, the Flower Garden Temple houses a fine 16th-century Buddha cast in bronze. This temple was the royal cemetery, and has many shrines containing the ashes of past kings.

Wat Jet Yod
In peaceful grounds on the highway that rings Chiang Mai, near the intersection with Kuay Kaew Road, the temple was built specially for the Eighth World Buddhist Council, held here in 1445. The "Seven Peaks" of its name refer to its seven *chedis* topping a square *viharn*. In front stands a large open-sided ordination hall, or *ubusot*. The laterite walls are sculpted with 70 heavenly beings, while outside are several images of Buddha—seated on one side, standing on the other.

You may be able to converse with the monks, who will be pleased to have the opportunity to practise their English.

National Museum
If you are planning an expedition into the hills to visit the mountain tribes, drop in first at the museum to view displays of objects and jewellery crafted by the Meo and the Akha, as well as some beautiful Buddhas.

Wat Gate
Located on Charoen Rat Road, on the east bank of the Ping River, this temple stands in the centre of a fascinating district where popular restaurants jostle with designer boutiques. The temple dates from the first half of the 15th century, at which time the river area in front of it was the town's port. Imposing garudas covered in mirror tiles guard the large *chedi*. To the east, the ordination hall *(ubusot)* is sculpted with all kinds of animals, from the horned nagas at the stairs to the main entrance to creatures from the Chinese zodiac in panels beneath the windows. The roof of the main prayer hall *(viharn)* has five gables (most temples have no more than three).

In an old building behind the *viharn* there's an interesting **museum** with collections ranging from the old flag of Siam, bearing a white elephant, to phonograph records and players, an antique wind-up victrola, and fascinating photographs showing scenes of Chiang Mai a century ago.

Night Bazaar

On Chang Klan Road, next to the Novotel, the night bazaar operates from 6 p.m. to 11 p.m. This is the best in the whole country, with a fabulous selection of silver jewellery, carved teak objects, parasols, clothing, silk ties, watches, fans and more. Shops, arcades and open-air stalls spread along both sides of the road; the atmosphere is easy-going and there are prices to suit every budget. And you're not likely to go hungry: there are excellent food stalls, too.

Warorot Market

Between Witchayanon Road and Chang Moi Road, this is the town's oldest market, specializing in fabrics.

Wat Phra That Doi Suthep

You can join an excursion to this place of pilgrimage 11 km (7 miles) west of town. On a mountain top, at an altitude of 1,676 m (5,500 ft) it affords wonderful views over the city and surrounding region. The temple stands at the top of a flight of 300 steps lined by *nagas*. According to legend, the site was chosen by a white elephant who had been charged with the task of finding a suitable location for keeping a hair from Buddha's head. At each corner of the *chedi* stands a delicately wrought gilded parasol.

Silk Workshops

You could spend a whole day pottering around the workshops lining the road to the small town of **San Kamphaeng**, 13 km (8 miles) east of Chiang Mai, known for its sericulture (the production of silk). In each workshop there is usually a guide to explain the various stages of manufacture before leaving you to browse.

Mae Rim

There are several orchid farms in the region of Mae Rim, 15 km (9 miles) northwest of Chiang Mai. **Sai Nam Phung** is one of the most popular, displaying some 35,000 species which flower at different times throughout the year. The tropical monsoon forests and mangrove swamps of Thailand provide ideal conditions for these exquisite plants. No fewer than 14 principles have to be carefully observed in their cultivation. There is also a butterfly farm here, where you can see gorgeous exotic species in their natural habitat.

Close by is the **Mae Sae elephant camp**, where every morning the trained elephants demonstrate their forestry skills. After the show, you can ride through the jungle on elephant back.

Chiang Dao

To enjoy a change of surroundings, visit the Chiang Dao elephant training camp, some 60 km (40 miles) north of Chiang Mai, halfway to Chiang Rai. Here nature reigns supreme, in the middle of a forest along the banks of the Ping River.

The place is rather too obviously designed with tourists in mind, but the show is well worth seeing. The elephants enter in single file, obeying the orders of their mahouts, who are often members of the Karen tribe. First, you'll see the elephants at their cheerful *toilette* in the river; then, from the tiered wooden seats, you'll watch the animals demonstrating log-rolling and teamwork.

Mae Hong Son

The road from Chiang Mai to the town of Mae Hong Son, 274 km (170 miles) to the northwest, meanders through jungle-clad mountains with craggy limestone peaks, dotted with high-perched villages. In the last little town on the road, **Pai**, you can hire a motorbike to better enjoy the last lap of the journey. Sometimes the roads dwindle into mere tracks hugging the contours of the mountains. And not a soul to be seen, apart from a peasant or two, from the Lisu or Lahu tribes, at work in the fields.

Founded in 1874 by the king of Chiang Mai, Mae Hong Son remained completely isolated from

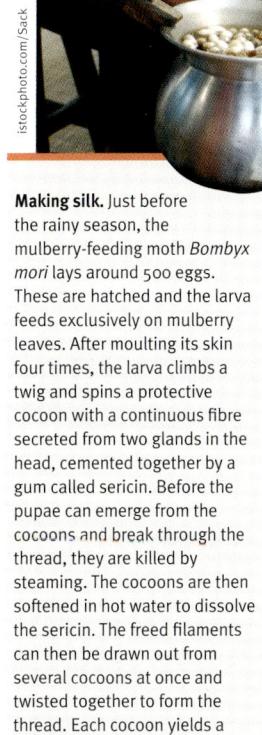

Making silk. Just before the rainy season, the mulberry-feeding moth *Bombyx mori* lays around 500 eggs. These are hatched and the larva feeds exclusively on mulberry leaves. After moulting its skin four times, the larva climbs a twig and spins a protective cocoon with a continuous fibre secreted from two glands in the head, cemented together by a gum called sericin. Before the pupae can emerge from the cocoons and break through the thread, they are killed by steaming. The cocoons are then softened in hot water to dissolve the sericin. The freed filaments can then be drawn out from several cocoons at once and twisted together to form the thread. Each cocoon yields a filament more than 500 m (1,500 ft) in length.

the rest of the country until 1965, when the road was finally built. Today it is the perfect place for resting a few days before or after a trekking holiday. There are several guesthouses overlooking a pretty lake busy with ducks and geese. The landscape is magnificent, with mountains and temples reflected in the still waters.

This is a small town, built around two main thoroughfares, and you may be taken aback to notice several banks, modern grocery stores and gleaming new four-wheel-drive vehicles driving up and down. That's because traffickers in precious stones, drugs, teak and other prohibited or strictly controlled substances come here for their food supplies. But it's a quiet place, and tourists are always made welcome.

The Thai Yai people indigenous to this region have developed a special architectural style adapted to the extremes of weather. Their homes have low roofs, single levels for the more humble house and multiple levels for local aristocrats. A typical feature of this style is a perforated design along the eaves.

Temples

The influence of nearby Myanmar is evident in the architecture of many of the temples and monasteries. The spires emerging from a coconut grove beside Nong Chong Kham lake belong to **Wat Chong Kham**, built by Thai Yai craftsmen in the early 19th century, and its neighbour **Wat Chong Klang**. Chom Kham has gilded pillars, a large Buddha statue cast by Burmese craftsmen, and a replica of the Wat Suthat Buddha in Bangkok. Chong Klang contains an unusual collection of 35 wooden polychrome figurines, or *tukatas*, representing characters described in the *jatakas* and brought here from Myanmar in 1857.

In **Wat Hua Wiang**, near the morning market, the Buddha image, Phra Chao Pharalakhaeng, is a replica of a statue in Mandalay.

On a hill to the west of town, at 424 m (1,400 ft), **Wat Phra That Doi Kong Mu** has two Burmese-style *chedis* dating from the late 19th century. There is a wonderful view over the region from here. The Thais come at the weekends to bring offerings.

Wat Phra Non lies at the foot of the hill; its Reclining Buddha, 12 m (39 ft) long, is in the Thai Yai style. Outside are two large sculpted lions, forming a passageway for pilgrims going up to the Kong Mu temple.

Hill-tribe Villages

Trips can be arranged from Mae Hong Son to visit a Padang village near the border with Myan-

POI SANG LONG FESTIVAL

Held in Mae Hong Son every year between March and May, the Poi Sang Long festival is the Thai Yai celebration of novice ordination. For three days, it brings together all the inhabitants of the town and its surrounding villages. Some families save for years to provide for this event.

Each young candidate, his head cleanly shaven, wears carefully applied make-up and is dressed in bejewelled, silken robes. Around his forehead is tied a wide band, studded with flowers. Often, the wealthiest family invites them all for a meal, providing the finest foods. Afterwards, the chosen young are paraded through the streets, borne on the shoulders of family members or on horseback to the city shrine, where they beg for forgiveness. The next day, the little princes are admitted to the monastery to lead the life of a novice monk for a month or more.

The festivities are a reminder that Buddha was a prince who lived in luxury before renouncing his wealth to seek the meaning of life and the rewards of asceticism.

Renata Holzbachová

mar. The Padang clan belongs to the Karen tribe. These are the "long-necked people", the women proudly wearing up to 25 brass rings around their necks and legs. Weighing on average 4 kg (9 lb), the rings do not stretch the neck but press down on and deform the shoulder muscles. It's said that this custom originated as a tribute to one of the tribe's ancestors, a female dragon. You will probably be charged a fee at the entrance to the village for the right to take photographs. Many visitors are shocked by this, but you should be aware that the money is shared with the Padang.

Living in bamboo huts in the middle of the jungle, the people seem quite contented with their lot; they lead a quiet life and don't suffer from want, which is more than can be said for many of the tribes living in northern Thailand.

Like many other ethnic groups originally from Myanmar, the Padang had to flee their country to escape abuse by Burmese soldiers. They are very welcoming and love to meet foreigners.

Descendants of the dragon spirits, the Padang women wear brass rings round their necks and legs. | Sunset on the River Kok, a tributary of the Mekong, near Chiang Rai.

You will probably see elephants at work in the Padang villages. The only means of transport between villages, the elephant is a robust worker and indispensable in the forest.

Chiang Rai

At equal distance from the borders with Laos and Myanmar, Chiang Rai is the southern tip of the Golden Triangle, in the heart of the mountains. An adventurous and roundabout way to reach the town is to drive to **Fang**, near the Myanmar border, then take a *hang yao* (long-tailed canoe) at the village of **Thaton**, and sail along the Nam Mae Kok river to Chiang Rai, a five- to six-hour journey. On the way, you can stop off in village inhabited by ethnic minorities, such as **Mae Salak** (Lahu) or **Ban Ruammit** (Karen), heralded by the trumpeting of elephants playing in the river.

Chiang Rai was founded in the 13th century by Mengrai, who later decided to make Chiang Mai his capital. Today the town has grown prosperous thanks to the tourist industry, but not so long ago it was a major centre for the poppyseed trade, now illegal. The ethnic minorities try to survive by cultivating the alternative crops promoted by the government.

Chiang Rai is the gateway for treks into the mountains; the surrounding landscape is untamed and unforgettable. But before you set off, take time to look around the 15th-century **Wat Phra Keo**: its *chedi* once sheltered Bangkok's Emerald Buddha.

When trekking, take care not to stray into Burmese territory. The border is unmarked, and you risk getting into trouble with the Myanmar military authorities.

Chiang Saen

Right on the border, on the banks of the Mekong, this village was once the capital of a principality. Some of its ruins date from the 10th century. In 1328, one of King Mengrai's grandsons had a new city built and incorporated into the kingdom of Lan Na. The Burmese invaded and used Chiang Saen as a base for launching attacks against the Thais. Later, Rama I destroyed the town to deny it to the Burmese. Today there are several temples and an interesting National Museum to visit.

Mae Sai

North of Chiang Rai, on the Myanmar border, Mae Sai has a lively and colourful market thanks to the presence of people coming from Myanmar, who just have to cross a bridge to enter Thailand. Occasionally the frontier is opened in the other direction, in which case you can visit the little town of **Tachilek**.

Akha women picking teea near Mae Salong in the north.

NORTHERN TRIBES

Most of the ethnic minorities you meet in the region of Chiang Mai, Mae Hong Son, Pai and Chiang Rai originally came from Tibet, China, Laos or Myanmar. In the past, they were able to slip easily through the frontier, which was poorly defined, and settle in Thailand. Today, government policy is to restrict the flow of migrants and to oblige the tribes to integrate. However, many refugees from Myanmar and Cambodia have increased their numbers in recent times. There are about 20 distinct tribes, the best-known being the Hmong, the Mien, the Lahu, the Akha, the Lisu and the Karen.

The Yao or Mien

Hailing from southern China, about 60,000 Yao (their Thai name) or Mien now live in Thailand, settled for the most part in the provinces of Nan and Chiang Rai. Living from crops grown on burnt stubble and from the sale of opium poppies, they practise Taoism and believe in the reincarnation of the soul. Often wearing an elegant black turban, a boa of red wool inside the jacket collar, and loose-fitting trousers, Yao women are renowned for their magnificent embroidery.

The Hmong or Meo

A people from China, the Hmong or Meo number about 150,000, concentrated in Chiang Mai province and along the frontier with Laos, from where they fled during the 1975 revolution. They are subdivided into White and Blue, according to the colour of their costumes. The men wear black jackets and baggy trousers, the women indigo skirts and jewellery, often knotting their hair into a thick chignon. Work in the fields is allotted to the women, who relax by smoking pipes. Hmong villages are always built above 1,200 m (4,000 ft), an altitude suitable for poppy cultivation, and often on a moderate slope to allow water supply by bamboo pipes. The wood houses are thatched. You will often see Hmong people selling jewellery in the night bazaar at Chiang Mai.

WOMEN OF THE NORTHERN HILL TRIBES

1, 2, 3, 4, 6 Renata Holzbachová / 5, Bernard Jolliat

These six groups are divided in turn into several sub-groups, each with its own dress and beliefs.

1 *Lisu*   2 *Meo*   3 *Akha*   4 *Yao*   5 *Karen*   6 *Lahu*

The Akha

The Akha first migrated from Yunnan in China to Myanmar, where they are still numerous in the region of Kengtung. There are about 70,000 in Thailand, mainly north of the River Kok, in villages always built at an altitude of more than 1,000 m (3,300 ft). The Akha grow rice and poppies. They are animists who worship their departed ancestors and appease their spirits with animal sacrifices. To enter an Akha village, you must pass through a wooden gate carved with prominent genitalia which are believed to ensure fertility and keep away evil spirits. Compared to the other tribes, the Akha are certainly the poorest and the most open. They are also the most light-hearted, loving festivals, during which they enjoy eating dog stew. The hardest work falls to the women, the men spending most of their time at home. Akha women wear elaborate headdresses lavishly decorated with silver ornaments and Indian coins, which often represent the entire wealth of the family. There are several styles corresponding to various origins: a sort of button-encrusted helmet for the Phami-Akha; a flat silver plaque behind the headdress for the Loimi-Akha; a plaque surmounting a cone covered in silver decoration for the U Lo-Akha. Often the silver ornaments are sold to buy rice or heroin and replaced by aluminium. Small, often in a hurry, and going barefoot, Akha women are usually dressed in a long-sleeved black and red jacket covered with silver decoration, a short, low-waisted skirt dyed with indigo, and leggings.

The Lisu

Of Tibeto-Burmese origin, the Lisu arrived in Thailand during the first half of the 20th century. They have had to make do with the highlands, up to 1,800 m (6,000 ft) above sea-level. There are about 25,000, living close to the Burmese border, cultivating rice and maize but deriving their main income from the poppy. The society is patriarchal, and a dowry system governs relations between men and women. The fiancé must assemble a considerable sum to marry his betrothed. The women wear a turban and long tunics in several colours (green, red, yellow and purple) over trousers; the men wear baggy trousers fastened at the ankle.

The Lahu

The Lahu are of Sino-Tibetan origin. They have been in Thailand since the 19th century and are consequently well assimilated. They number more than 60,000 and live in villages at 1,000 m

(3,300 ft). The Lahu have the reputation of being excellent hunters and skilful musicians. They cultivate poppies. For the most part, they are animists, but there are a few Christian communities. The older Lahu still wear traditional costume; the women dressing in long black jackets with red embroidery and silver ornaments, the men in green and blue trousers.

The Karen

Originally from Myanmar, this tribe numbers some 300,000 and has been settled in Thailand longer than all the other hill tribes. They cultivate rice and live mostly in the region of Mae Hong Son, in villages established at a fairly low altitude — 500 m (1,600 ft). Their society is endogamous and matriarchal, women inheriting property, the men devoting themselves essentially to training elephants.

Evangelized by American preachers in the 19th century and later by Christian missionaries, the Karen have adopted very strict rules of life and consume neither alcohol nor heroin. The women are skilled weavers. Energetic and talented in business, the Karen are well integrated into rural life and often occupy positions of responsibility.

Poppies. Their villages often being in mountain regions where the soil is not sufficiently fertile to grow rice on a large scale, the minorities, with the notable exception of the Karen, survived sinc the 19th century by growing opium poppies which they sold to drug traffickers. Today, the Thai government is trying to put a stop to this practice but it is not an easy task. Growing was made illegal in 1959, and a cash crop substitution programme was introduced in the 1990s. However, production has surged since 2006. Traditionally, poppies were cultivated to give ease to the elderly during their last days. The poppy *(Papaver somniferum)* is grown on burnt stubble in the mountains. Seeding is in April and the harvest is gathered between the end of December and the beginning of March, when the fruit is in the form of a green capsule. The head of the fruit is cut with a stylet, allowing the flow of a white sap which browns on contact with the air. This "gum" is then boiled and purified to obtain a brown paste ready for consumption. The Chinese serve as intermediaries between the tribes and the traffickers.

THE KAREN AND THEIR ELEPHANTS

For the Karen, the elephant is part of the family. Even better—it is a "rice-winner", employed at transporting tourists and tree trunks. Families have to save their money for many a long year to gather enough to buy an elephant, which can live to the age of 60.

As a rule, a female will produce only four young in her lifetime, so a pregnancy is a great event. From the first signs, she is installed in the area reserved for the calves where she will enjoy a long maternity leave—24 months of pregnancy followed by three years to look after her baby. The first years of an elephant's life are the happiest: for three years he has nothing to do but fill his stomach with everything he can chew, with a preference for bananas and sugar cane.

The calf is attended 24 hours a day by his mahout, who spends at least five years with it at the training centre. Gradually, a bond develops between the man and the animal. After "primary school", the pupils graduate to a "trade school" apprenticeship and are taught to roll, lift and push tree trunks. The training can take up to ten years.

The first command they learn is *peh-peh* (lie down). Morning ablutions occur in a cloud of dust as the animals constantly squirt themselves with sand and earth to drive away the flies. After a check-up, the elephants rush off for a bath, after which they start work. When school is over for the day, it is time for play and refreshments. The mahouts take their young charges into the forest, every day to a different place, because elephants love young shoots. By the end of the dry season between March and May, the forest around the training camp is completely devastated. Consequently, the elephants are given a holiday, to go off to a distant part of the forest. To gather their strength, elephants sleep standing up from around 9 p.m. to 5 a.m. or earlier.

Renata Holzbachová

Fruit and vegetables are beautifully sculpted for table decorations.

DINING OUT

Apart from pastries and the use of the fork imported from England in the 19th century by King Chulalongkorn, Western food has little influence in Thai cuisine. Thais are past masters of the culinary arts and have a simple philosophy with regard to food—"Eat when you are hungry".

To put this into practice, nowhere better than the street stalls which serve tasty dishes at all hours. Their cuisine is tasty, often spicy, and always healthy. The basic ingredients are pork, chicken, beef, crab, shrimp and fish, all lifted to gastronomic realms by the use of sauces and chillies. If you have a sensitive stomach, you can always ask for milder dishes in restaurants.

Food, Glorious Food
The Thais love eating, and happily, they are also good cooks. Day and night (till about 10 p.m.), some of the streets in Bangkok, in Chiang Mai, indeed in almost every large town, are packed with street vendors preparing tantalizing heaps of fried bananas, crispy Peking duck, hot curries, and so on. The best way to deal with the situation is to stroll around tasting here and there as the fancy takes you, guided by your nose.

Even monks and nuns succumb to the pleasures of the table. Don't be under the illusion that all monks have to beg for their daily rations every morning and are satisfied with a simple bowl of rice. You have only to spend a few nights as a guest in certain monasteries in the Bangkok suburbs to see how far that is from the truth—and to observe the battalions of nuns who spend their time cooking and serving the fortunate monks with countless dishes, each finer than the last.

A Typical Meal
The typical Thai meal is composed of a great variety of dishes—soups, salads (*yam*), curried fish and meat—set out all together on the table along with the traditional bowl of steamed white rice *(kow na)*. Diners take a spoonful of this and that as they wish. Several sauces are presented, such as the spicy fish

sauce *nam pla prik*. Rice is the staple food here and accompanies curries, beef, pork, sautéed chicken, duck—just about everything.

Some Like It Hot

A whole range of chillies is available. The hottest is small in size, orange in colour and strong in sensation—*prik kee nu luang*. If you are taken unawares and fall victim to its fearsome properties, swallow some plain boiled white rice to extinguish the burning sensation.

Seasoning is provided by *nam pla*, a fermented fish sauce, *nam yam hai,* oyster sauce, or *nam king*, ginger sauce, among others. Meats and fish are often spiced with a mixture of salt, pepper, coriander, garlic, basil and cardamom, all ground up together in a mortar.

From South to North

Whereas curries predominate in the south, the most varied and delicious cooking is found in Bangkok. You can eat Indian, Indonesian and especially Chinese, with those scrumptious little bites of steamed *dim sum* and the supreme Peking duck.

Traditional food in Chiang Mai is less highly spiced than that served in the central plains. In the north, people eat sticky rice, sometimes rolled into little balls. A pleasant way of tasting northern cuisine is to take part in a *kantoke* dinner, a sort of traditional banquet. You sit on the floor before a low bamboo table on which several dishes are served, including *pik kai yang* (chicken wings) and *sai krok* (sausages) with sticky rice. The atmosphere is always jolly, with dancing and music.

Specialities

Here are a few of the dishes which you won't regret ordering: *tom yam kung* (shrimp soup with mushrooms and lemon grass); *satay* (barbecued skewers of meat served with a spicy peanut sauce); *mee kha ti* (rice vermicelli in coconut milk); *kow pat* (fried rice); *pat thai* (fried rice noodles); *kai tot* (grilled chicken). Don't miss the fish salad (*yam pla*) or green papaya salad (*som tam*).

If you want to pick up some ideas, you can watch the chef at work in the kitchen. See, for example, how they prepare chicken in coconut milk: boil the chicken pieces in hot vegetable stock for three minutes, then stir in the seasoned milk. Easy and delicious!

Desserts and Fruit

Thais always finish a meal with fruit. The colourful markets offer a staggering variety of fruit at derisory prices: coconuts, mangoes, mangosteens, bananas, custard apples, rambutans, lychees, jackfruit, starfruit, cantaloup melons, papayas and tamarind, recommended for intestinal problems. Their presentation is an art in Thailand.

You must taste the delicious flans made of coconut and the sweet cakes wrapped in banana leaves. If you have a craving for cheese, then try replacing it by the durian, a fruit with a prickly skin but whose flesh is pronounced exquisite by the Thais. The smell of the durian has been compared with everything pungent from rotting onions to sweaty socks; they are banned from some hotels and aircraft.

Drinks

With such a wealth of fruit, you willl be never be at a loss for refreshing juices. In the evenings, try the local beer (Singha), not bad at all. A word of advice: avoid strong alcohol and the deceptive Thai whisky known as Mekong—in the heat, it could well spoil your holiday.

Some tempting culinary specialities: noodle soup with shrimp; dried fish; spicy chicken satay. | Be adventurous and discover some exotic fruit such as the luscious mangosteen with its sweet and tangy flesh.

Countless species of orchid are grown in Thailand.

SHOPPING

It would be ideal to arrive in Bangkok with empty bags. And the first day, on Khao San Road in the touristic area of Banglamphu, to fill up your summer wardrobe for next to nothing: T shirts, trousers, skirts and sandals for a carefree holiday. And don't forget a spare suitcase to fill up with gifts for your friends and family.

There is no lack of choice. There are markets everywhere. Crafts are of high quality and not at all expensive. Two places that must not be missed: Chiang Mai in the north, and Khao San Road in Bangkok. But before you buy anything, check the weight limits for your return flight; it would be a pity to have to pay extra taxes.

The list of bargains is long: CDs, DVDs, watches, suitcases, rucksacks, scarves, jewellery, decorated fans, toys, items in leather or wood, pens, clothing, greetings cards, basketwork. As well as orchids, spices, and why not a wok to try your hand at Thai cuisine when you get back home. Paper lanterns, like those sent up into the sky at Chiang Mai for the November Loi Kratong (Festival of Lights) are easy to carry (they fold up).

If you enjoy searching for that elusive dream bargain, then it is almost sure that you will spend most of your evenings in Thailand browsing around the irresistible markets, shopping centres, handicraft shops and street stalls. There are some lovely items to be found at relatively low prices, partly because of cheap labour, the availability of counterfeit goods and the Thais' good taste.

If anyone tries to convince you that a particular item is either antique or authentic, take it with a pinch of salt. Haggle if you wish, but don't overdo it—the Thais can be quite fearsome when annoyed.

Antiques
It is illegal to export antiques, which are liable to be seized by customs officers. Nevertheless, there are some good bargains to be had in Bangkok in the district around the Oriental Hotel: bronzes and wooden Buddhas. But watch your step.

Parasols. The brightly coloured parasols, all made by hand, are irresistible, even if the only use you will have for them back home is to add a touch of exoticism to your interior decoration. The best-known parasol workshop is at Bo Sang, 9 km (6 miles) east of Chiang Mai. They have been making parasols here for at least two centuries, using only local materials.

Producing a parasol requires real teamwork: one group carves the wooden handles and assembles the bamboo ribs, then young women stretch the cotton, silk or brown paper (made from mulberry bark) over the frame, and finally another group applies the painted decoration. Some of the parasols are left plain, in vibrant colours, others are decorated with attractive floral motifs.

Crafts

World-renowned, Thai silk (as well as cotton) is mostly made in the region of Chiang Mai, the capital of handicrafts in Thailand. San Kamphaeng Road is lined with numerous workshops and sales outlets. You can watch the whole silk-making process from the cultivtion of silkworms to the finished product.

Karalas are embroidered Burmese tapestries, usually representing epic scenes involving elephants. Most are made today around Mandalay in Myanmar, though the vendor will try to persuade you that they are authentic antiques.

Lacquered objects, stencilled with gold leaf, are usually superb. The lacquer comes from the sap of *Melanorrhea usitata*, a tree which grows in the mountains.

Celadon (green ceramic) pots are very decorative, as are the bamboo and teak items.

As you travel around, you'll see women from the Akha or Yao mountain tribes selling fabrics, bracelets and other jewellery made by their families. They are always gracious and smiling.

Made to Measure

If you've always hankered after a tailored suit made to fit you perfectly, you'll find the answer to your dreams here, in Bangkok or any other city with facilities for tourists. The tailors are usually from India.

First you will choose the fabric. Then you will be carefully measured. Within a few days you can try on the garments (sometimes they may be brought to your hotel) and the final adjustments will be made to hems and seams before the finished suit is delivered.

Don't forget to try on ready-made silk and cotton clothing before you buy.

Precious stones

Bangkok jewellers are reputed for their skill in cutting and mounting sapphires and rubies, generally extracted in Myanmar. Semi-precious stones such as amethysts, garnets and jade also come from Myanmar. Emeralds may have been imported from South America and cats' eye, a variety of chrysoberyl, comes from Sri Lanka. Bear in mind that fakes are very common.

The sapphire mines near Chantaburi, 150 km (93 miles) southeast of Pattaya, are famed the world over. Thais flock to the sapphire market, held at weekends.

Heat from the candle flame send the lantern up to heaven. | **Working on a lacquered vase.** | **A vast array of woven fabrics.**

For a good start to the day, there's nothing like a tai chi session!

SPORTS

Travel by air or by coach in Thailand is so convenient that you could easily combine a two- or three-day walking tour in the north from Chiang Mai with a week of relaxation in the south on the sandy beaches. Dedicated athletes never miss the famous triathlon is held every year in mid-May on the beaches of Cha Am.

Hiking

Many agencies organize walking tours from Chiang Mai, usually including a visit to villages inhabited by mountain tribes. The best season is from November to February. From the month of March onwards the heat is unbearable, and in July and August rainfall is particularly heavy.

Before choosing an agent, it is wise to ask someone who has already been on a tour, and to ensure that your guide speaks reasonable English—or you could be in for a surprise. As for the mountain tribes you will meet, it is better to offer them medical supplies (such as aspirin) and pencils or crayons for the children, rather than giving them money. If you intend to sleep in villages, you'll probably find that a light, thick foam rubber mattress will come in handy. If you go river rafting, insist on being given a lifejacket.

There are also several popular, well-marked hiking trails in Khao Yai national park , which lies just east of Saraburi, northeast of Bangkok.

Water Sports

With 2,710 km (1,683 miles) of coastline and a dozen National Maritime Parks, you can go diving, sailing and big-game fishing all year round.

Sailing

In the west, the spectacular coast of the Andaman Sea stretches for 870 km (540 miles). Between the Tarutao Maritime Park, 5 km (3 miles) from the island of Langkawi in Malaysia, and the Surin Maritime Park, close to the Myanmar border, there is a host of small unspoiled islands. The Andaman Sea is deep and limpid. The water temperature varies between 26 and 28°C (79 and 82°F). The wind speed is never less than 5 knots and can reach 25 or 30 knots. Between April and October, the sea is rougher, with squalls and waves of up to 4 m (13 ft).

Phuket is a major centre for sailing, offering excursions to the islands of Ko Phi Phi, Surin or Similan, in the direction of Ao Phang Nga, north of Phuket. The weather is perfect from November until mid-May. Phang Nga Bay itself, sheltered from the winds, offers year-round boating within a huge natural stretch of water covering 400 sq km (154 sq miles) scattered with 40 or more little islands. There are yachts for hire with or without a crew. The traditional King's Cup Regatta is held around Phuket at the beginning of December and attracts skilled yachtsmen from all over Asia.

The Gulf of Thailand forms a bay 1,840 km (1,140 miles) long, and the China Sea is warm all year round, with a temperature varying between 26 and 30°C (79 and 86°F). The clear water offers good visibility for underwater fishing. High season is from May to October, when the skies are clear and the sea calm.

Sailors will want to head for Pattaya and the seaside resort of Jomtien where there are several marinas and yacht clubs. Sailing is possible all year round, and Bangkok is only two hours away by road. If you are looking for quieter moorings, then choose Ko Samui.

Diving

In the region around the Similan Islands, the sea is teeming with marine life, including splendid sea-fans and sponges. At depths of 5 or 6 m (16 to 20 ft), in magnificent coral gardens, whalesharks and manta rays come close inshore at the end of March when the plankton is abundant.

Another divers' paradise is Ko Chang National Park, southwest of Ranong in the Andaman Sea. High season is from November to mid-May.

Diving cruises are also available from Ko Tao in the Gulf of Thailand, where the underwater life is superb. Prices are very reasonable compared with Europe.

Fishing

On the Gulf of Thailand side, Pattaya has two centres which are very well equipped for big-game fishing. At the beginning of the year, fishermen can catch fine sailfish. In the Andaman Sea, the sailfish season lasts from mid-May until November. In July and August, you can be fairly certain of coming across tuna, barracudas and emperor fish.

Thai fishermen catch shark at night, using lantern-light around the Similan Islands. Enthusiasts

won't want to miss the traditional November fishing competition at Krabi. November to May is the season for tuna and marlin. Expeditions lasting from two to five days are organized between the Similan Islands and Phuket. On Phuket, specially equipped boats are based in Chalong Marina. You can explore the deep waters at about 2.5 hours' sailing time south from Phuket, and you may be lucky enough to haul in a yellow tuna or a black marlin weighing up to 200 kg (450 lb).

Windsurfing

Experienced windsurfers head for the west coast of Phuket between November and February, when the winds can reach 20 or 25 knots. Beginners prefer Kata or Karon beaches between April and October when the winds are more moderate. In the Gulf of Thailand, Jomtien Beach south of Pattaya is swept by stiff breezes between November and January. On Ko Samui, Bophut and Maenam, beaches are good all year round, while at Lamai and Chaweng in the east, windsurfing is dangerous between October and May during the monsoon.

Canoeing

You don't have to be an expert to enjoy the delights of floating in an inflatable canoe on the balmy waters of Ao Phang Nga.

Where traditional and modern can happily co-exist.

THE HARD FACTS

Airports
Suvarnabhumi international airport lies 30 km (19 miles) east of Bangkok in Racha Thewa, along the Chon Buri Highway. Airport facilities include car hire, pharmacy and duty-free shop, and 24-hour first aid, banks, bar, post office and nursery. The airport handles international and domestic flights.

The airport is linked to the City Air Terminal at Makkasan in central Bangkok in 15 minutes by express train (SARL, Suvarnabhumi Airport Rail Link). Other options include a shuttle bus, the public bus or taxis. There is a direct coach service to Pattaya.

Chiang Mai International Airport is 15 km (9 miles) from the city. Taxis are available.

Phuket International Airport lies 35 km (22 miles) northwest of Phuket. There are buses and taxis to the city centre.

Domestic flights also land at Hat Yai airport; it is 20 km (12 miles) from Songkhla.

A small departure tax is charged for domestic flights.

Border Crossing
If you hire a motorbike or a car or if you are hiking in the north, make sure you have your passport and take care not to cross the border into Myanmar. The Burmese army is not renowned for its hospitality.

Climate
The most comfortable season (neither too hot nor too humid) for visiting Thailand is from December to March. Rainfall drenches Bangkok in October and the sun is baking in April. The beaches in the south are pleasant all year round.

Communications
For local calls from a public phone you will need to buy a phone card. International calls can be made from public phone booths—but only from those with the international card phone logo. You can also call from the Telecom Building next to the Central Post Office in Bangkok, open 24 hours a day. In other cities, go to any large post office. You will also see street stalls set up by young people offering the services of their personal mobile phone, at a very cheap rate per minute.

The country code for Thailand is 66. To call a number in Bangkok from another province in Thailand, dial 02 then the number; to call other provinces from Bangkok there is no area code.

There are plenty of Internet cafés in the cities, often with scanning and printing facilities. Web access tends to be slow but it is not very expensive.

Courtesy

The vast majority of Thais are tolerant and genuinely hospitable towards foreigners so long as the latter respect certain customs. Never show disrespect to the monarchy, the king or the royal family. In temples, dress modestly and avoid showing your arms or legs. In some places, such as the Temple of the Emerald Buddha in Bangkok, you will be given trousers and long-sleeved shirt at the entrance if you are wearing shorts and T-shirt. Remove your shoes when entering a home or any building housing a statue of Buddha and never climb onto the statue. It is better to never adopt a position where you look down on a Buddha. In addition, women must not enter a monastery or anywhere inhabited by monks and must not touch a monk.

As far as morals are concerned, prostitution and special massages have long been recognized and accepted by the Thais. In some of the fashionable hotels of the capital it is commonplace for a man to be offered the services of an escort. In everyday life, however, Thais cultivate and appreciate discreet behaviour and modesty in dress. Thai women bathe in trousers and T-shirt rather than in a bathing costume. Expect to be politely ejected if you try to enter the Oriental Hotel in trainers.

Currency

The monetary unit is the baht, divided into 100 satang. Coins are issued in denominations of 25 and 50 satang (little used) and 1, 5 and 10 baht; banknotes of 20, 50, 100, 500 and 1,000 baht.

American Express, MasterCard and Visa cards are widely accepted in Bangkok and you can use them to withdraw money. However, in regions less frequented by tourists, it is wise to take US dollars or euros which can be exchanged in local hotels for baht.

Entry Formalities

A passport valid for at least six months after your departure is all you need for a stay of maximum 30 days. For a longer visit, you will need a visa.

You are allowed to import, duty-free, 200 cigarettes or 250 g cigars or 250 g tobacco, as well as 1 litre wine or spirits. You can import and export up to 50,000 baht; there are no restrictions on import or export of foreign currency.

Electricity

The electric current is 220 volts AC, 50 Hz. Generally 2-pin plugs are used. Don't forget to take an adaptor for your mobile phone and camera battery chargers.

Health

Thailand has good medical facilities, especially in Bangkok. Avoid drinking tap water or eating raw, unpeeled fruit and vegetables. The biggest problem encountered by foreigners arriving in Thailand is a sore throat caused by the chilly air conditioning in the hotels and shopping malls. Any chemist will give advice for a suitable over-the-counter medication. They also sell the best products to keep the mosquitoes at bay. In the tropical forest, out in the country and in some of the southern islands, mosquitoes carry a severe form of malaria.

Be careful also when sitting under the palm trees—it is possible to be killed by falling coconuts. Rabies is present, even in Bangkok. Avoid stroking stray dogs, cats and other animals.

Something else that you may find annoying is the noise, and not only loud music. It's a good idea to take earplugs.

Holidays and Festivals

Banks and businesses close on the following days:

January 1	*New Year's Day*
April 6	*Chakri Day*
May 1	*Labour Day*
May 5	*Coronation Day*
August 12	*Queen's Birthday*
October 23	*Chulalongkorn Day*
December 5	*King's Birthday*
December 10	*Constitution Day*
December 31	*New Year's Eve*

Chinese New Year (moveable) is partly observed.

The week from December 28 to January 2 is high season for the Thais who flock to the beaches. If you want to visit during this period, make your hotel bookings well ahead.

Songkran, the Thai New Year, is celebrated in April.

Loi Kratong, held in November, is a delightful occasion. The *kratong* is a little banana-leaf boat carrying a single lighted candle and floated on the rivers and lakes to thank Buddha and the water spirits. It is a magical spectacle in the dark, especially on the Chao Phraya in Bangkok, in Chiang Mai and Sukothai. You may also see lanterns sent up into the sky, like miniature hot-air balloons.

Language

Thai is a tonal language and very difficult for a foreigner to learn. English is fairly widespread in the touristic areas. Ask someone at your hotel reception desk to write down the hotel's name in

Thai, and the address of the places you want to go. Taxi and *tuk-tuk* drivers rarely speak anything other than Thai. Before hiring a guide, make sure that he speaks reasonable English.

Newspapers

The English-language daily *The Nation* concentrates on national news, while *The Bangkok Post* is more international, and has the local weather forecast on page 2. Its supplement, *Outlook*, sometimes carries interesting magazine articles. See also the site www.onlinenewspapers.com/thailand.htm

Opening Hours

Banks generally open Monday to Friday 9.30 a.m.–3.30 p.m. in Bangkok and from 8.30 a.m. elsewhere.

Museums open 9 a.m.–4.30 or 5 p.m.

Shops are often open 12 hours a day, 7 days a week. The big stores in Bangkok close at 8 p.m.

Post offices close at 4.30 or 5 p.m. Bangkok's main post office, on New Road, opens Monday to Friday 7.30 a.m.–4.30 p.m., Saturdays and public holidays 9 a.m.–noon.

Photography

If you are still using standard film, store it in the refrigerator of your hotel room, inside a plastic bag. Avoid taking photos at midday when the sun is very high: the morning and evening light is much better. Ask for permission before taking photos of people; sometimes they may ask for a fee.

Security

Thailand is a very safe country for travellers. Theft and mugging are rare.

Time

The time, year round, is GMT+7. When it is noon in the UK, it is 7 p.m. in winter in Thailand and 6 p.m. in summer.

Tipping

Thais never give tips, but the custom has now taken root in the tourism business. If you are planning to go north and hike through villages inhabited by mountain tribes, you might like to take small gifts for the children such as coloured pencils.

Toilets

In general, clean toilets are available in hotels and restaurants.

Transport

In Bangkok, the gleaming new elevated BTS Skytrain will save you hours of frustration in the traffic; it covers much of the city apart from the Grand Palace and the river banks. It operates from 6 a.m. to midnight; trains run every 3 to 6 minutes. One-day passes are available for unlimited travel, as well as 30-day student or adult passes for 10, 15 or 30 trips. A quick way to reach the Grand Palace is to take the Skytrain to Saphan Taksin station south of the river, then one of the rapid boats.

The Blue Line of the Bangkok Subway opened in July 2004. With 18 stations, it runs from Bang Sue to Hua Lamphong, with connections to the Skytrain at Si Lom/Sala Daeng, Sukhumvit/ Asok and Chatuchak/Mo Chit. Extensions are planned.

The Chao Phraya Tourist Boat has 10 main stops, including the Oriental Hotel, Chinatown, Wat Arun, Wat Po, Grand Palace, Temple of the Emerald Buddha, Royal Barge Museum and the Bangalumpoo District. It runs from 9.30 a.m. to 3 p.m., departures every 30 minutes from Sathorn Pier (south). The sights are commented in English; day tickets available.

The most convenient way of getting from one city to another is by air. To compare prices see:
Thai Airways
(www.thaiairways.com),
Bangkok Airways
(www.bkkair.co.th)

Trains are sometimes slow, but the sleeping cars on long-distance trains are quite comfortable. But it can be more interesting to travel by coach; companies are numerous and you'll have no trouble finding a seat. During the warm season, make sure you choose a coach with air-conditioning.

A number of hotels and guesthouses in the district of Banglamphu (Kao San Road) organize excursions by minibus to Chiang Mai, the south and into Cambodia. There are departures every day, but the timetables are a bit haphazard.

The best way to see the northern areas from Chiang Mai, Chiang Rai or Mae Hong Son is by motorbike, and it's also an excellent means of getting around the islands Ko Samui, Ko Pha Ngan and Phuket. With some companies you will have to leave your passport, your driving licence and a deposit. Make sure you note down the phone number of the company or the owner of the vehicle, in case of police checks. Drive with great care. Accidents are very common, especially on Phuket. And you must have international insurance. Traffic drives on the left.

Here are some road distances from Bangkok:
Ayutthaya: 86 km
Chiang Mai: 700 km
Chiang Rai: 823 km
Hua Hin: 230 km
Pattaya: 140 km
Phuket: 922 km
Sukhothai: 466 km

INDEX

Ancient City see Muang Boran
Ang Thong National Marine Park 39
Ayutthaya 27–29
Bangkok 15–32
  amulet market 23
  Chao Phraya 21–23
  Chatuchak Market 25
  Chinese Quarter 22
  Democracy Monument 23
  Emerald Buddha see Wat Phra Kaeo
  Grand Palace 17
  Jim Thompson's House 25
  Nakhon Kasem 22
  National Gallery 21
  – **Museum** 20–21
  – **Theatre** 21
  Patpong 25–26
  Philatelic Museum 25
  Ratchadamnoen Stadium 23
  Royal Barge Museum 21
  Snake Farm 25
  Soi Cowboy 25–26
  Suan Pakkad Palace 24–25
  Thanon Kao San 23
  Traditional Theatre 20
  Vimanmek Mansion Museum 24
  Wat Arun 21–22
  – **Benchamabophit** 23–24
  – **Pho** 19–20
  – **Phra Kaeo** 17–18
  – **Saket** 23
  – **Suthat** 23
  – **Traimit** 22
Bang Pa-In 26–27
Bhumibol Dam 53
Bridge on the River Kwai 31
Cha Am 35–36
Chiang Dao 58–59
Chiang Mai 55–58
Chiang Rai 63
Chiang Saen 63
Damnoen Saduak 31
Hat Jomtien 34
Hat Naklua 34
Hill tribe villages 60–63
Hua Hin 37
Kaeng Krachan National Park 37–38
Kanchanaburi 31
Khao Lak 49
Khao Sam Roi Yot National Park 38
Ko Chang 35
Ko Kret 26
Ko Lanta 42–43
Ko Larn (Ko Lan) 34–35
Ko Pha Ngan 39
Ko Phi Phi 42
Ko Samet 35
Ko Samui 38–39
Ko Tao 39
Krabi 41–42
Lampang 55
Lamphun 55
Mae Hong Son 59–60
Mae Rim 58
Mae Sa elephant camp 58
Mae Sai 63
Mini Siam 34
Muang Boran 34
Nakhon Pathom 31
Nakhon Ratchasima 51
Nakhon Si Thammarat 41
Nong Nooch Village 34
Pai 59
Pattaya 33–34
Phang Nga 43–44
Phimai 51
Phitsanulok 53
Phuket 44–49
Phuket Town 44–47
Prasat Phanom Rung 51
Ratchaburi 31
Rayong 35
Rose Garden 29
Samut Prakan Crocodile Farm 29
San Kamphaeng 58
Silk Workshops 58
Songkran 56
Sukhothai 52–53
Surat Thani 38
Surin 51–52
Tak 53
Wat Prathat That Phanom 52

General editor
Barbara Ender-Jones

Editor
Christina Grisewood

English adaptation
Judith Farr

Design
Karin Palazzolo

Layout
Luc Malherbe

Photo credits
p. 1: Renata Holzbachová;
p. 2: istockphoto.com/Havet (orchid),
istockphoto.com/Erdmann (elephant),
istockphoto.com/Teo (statues of Buddha),
istockphoto.com/Vige (rock)

Maps
JPM Publications, Mathieu Germay

Copyright © 2010, 2000
JPM Publications S.A.
12, avenue William-Fraisse,
1006 Lausanne, Switzerland
information@jpmguides.com
http://www.jpmguides.com/

All rights reserved. No part of this book may be reproduced or transmitted in any form or by any means, electronic or mechanical, including photocopying, recording or by any information storage and retrieval system without permission in writing from the publisher.

Every care has been taken to verify the information in the guide, but the publisher cannot accept responsibility for any errors that may have occurred. If you spot an inaccuracy or a serious omission, please let us know.

Printed in Switzerland
12418.00.6727
Swissprinters IRL, Lausanne
Edition 2010